Sexology: The Basics is a wonderful introduction to what we know about sex from research, theory, and therapeutic practice. Packed full of interesting facts, thoughtful reflection, and real-world examples, Silva has done a brilliant job of gathering together current knowledge and presenting it in a super accessible and engaging form. Each chapter ends with helpful questions we can ask ourselves, and signposts for how we can find out more. An inclusive and entertaining read, that highlights the diversity of sexual identities, desires, practices, and more.

Meg-John Barker, *author of* Sexuality: A Graphic Guide

This book is a positive, normalising and informative contribution to us all learning more about sexology. Silva clearly explains the biopsychosocial approach to sexology with all of the moving parts that contribute to our sexual wellness. It offers context, both historical and current, explaining the current sexual and relationship landscape we live in today. Silva asks us to consider our own biases and position as a reader, in order to be more informed as professionals.

Kate Moyle, *EFS & ESSM Certified Psycho-Sexologist & Host of Podcast: The Sexual Wellness Sessions*

This book is an absolute triumph! Silva shares his clinical expertise in a way that feels so accessible, there's a rich array of information, all presented with kindness and enthusiasm. He covers a broad range of topics to provide foundational information about his field, as well as looking at the ways in which sex and relationships can play out in the wider context of our lives. A must read for everyone interested in the world of sexology.

Ruby Rare, *author of* Sex Ed: A Guide for Adults

Not to be pigeonholed into one area of clinical sexology (his book on compulsive sexual behaviour is a best seller and core text on many courses), but he has produced another fine book within a year of publication. I loved the breadth of content and the clarity and ease of approaching contemporary sexology. Still, most of all, I enjoyed the case vignettes which beautifully illustrate his key concepts.

Dominic Davies, *Psychotherapist, Sexologist and Founder of Pink Therapy*

SEXOLOGY

Sexology: The Basics is the contemporary manual of human sexuality, eroticism, and intimate relationships. It takes you to every corner of the human erotic mind and physiological arousal response for a thorough understanding of all the functional parts of our sexualities, including how we bond, love, and have sex from a broad perspective of diversities in sex, gender, and relationships, from monogamy to polyamory, Vanilla to Kink. This book is bridges the gaps in our knowledge of sex education.

It is the ultimate guide to answering all the questions you never dared to ask, whether you are a student or a professional, or want to make sense of our often confusing erotic world.

Silva Neves is a COSRT-accredited and UKCP-registered psychotherapist specialising in sexology and intimate relationships. He is a Course Director for the Contemporary Institute of Clinical Sexology (CICS), an international speaker, broadcaster, and an author.

THE BASICS

The Basics is a highly successful series of accessible guidebooks which provide an overview of the fundamental principles of a subject area in a jargon-free and undaunting format.

Intended for students approaching a subject for the first time, the books both introduce the essentials of a subject and provide an ideal springboard for further study. With over 50 titles spanning subjects from artificial intelligence (AI) to women's studies, *The Basics* are an ideal starting point for students seeking to understand a subject area.

Each text comes with recommendations for further study and gradually introduces the complexities and nuances within a subject.

SKEPTICISM
JUAN COMESAÑA AND MANUEL COMESAÑA

FILM THEORY (second edition)
KEVIN MCDONALD

SEMIOTICS (fourth edition)
DANIEL CHANDLER

CHOREOGRAPHY
JENNY ROCHE AND STEPHANIE BURRIDGE

ENVIRONMENTAL AND ARCHITECTURAL PSYCHOLOGY
IAN DONALD

NEW RELIGIOUS MOVEMENTS
JOSEPH LAYCOCK

AIR POLLUTION AND CLIMATE CHANGE
JOHN PEARSON AND RICHARD DERWENT

LANGUAGE ACQUISITION
PAUL IBBOTSON

INFANCY
MARC H. BORNSTEIN AND MARTHA E. ARTERBERRY

PHILOSOPHY OF RELIGION
SAMUEL LEBENS

SEX THERAPY
CATE CAMPBELL

CLASSICAL MYTHOLOGY
RICHARD MARTIN

SOCIAL WORK
MARK DOEL

For more information about this series, please visit: www.routledge.com/The-Basics/book-series/B

SEXOLOGY

THE BASICS

Silva Neves

Routledge
Taylor & Francis Group

LONDON AND NEW YORK

Cover image: Getty Images

First published 2023
by Routledge
4 Park Square, Milton Park, Abingdon, Oxon OX14 4RN

and by Routledge
605 Third Avenue, New York, NY 10158

Routledge is an imprint of the Taylor & Francis Group, an informa business

© 2023 Silva Neves

British Library Cataloguing-in-Publication Data
A catalogue record for this book is available from the British Library

ISBN: 978-1-032-23363-5 (hbk)
ISBN: 978-1-032-23362-8 (pbk)
ISBN: 978-1-003-27691-3 (ebk)

DOI: 10.4324/9781003276913

Typeset in Bembo
by SPi Technologies India Pvt Ltd (Straive)

CONTENTS

BIOGRAPHY

Silva Neves

Silva Neves is a COSRT-accredited and UKCP-registered psycho-sexual and relationship psychotherapist, a trauma psychotherapist, and a clinical supervisor. He is a Pink Therapy Clinical Associate.

Silva is Course Director for CICS (Contemporary Institute of Clinical Sexology), an international speaker, broadcaster, and an author.

Silva is a member of the editorial board for the leading international journal *Sex and Relationship Therapy*.

Silva is the author of *Compulsive Sexual Behaviours, A Psycho-Sexual Treatment Guide for Clinicians* (2021, Routledge).

ACKNOWLEDGEMENTS

A book is never written in isolation. I'm so grateful for the outstanding professional network I'm a part of. First of all, I would like to thank my colleague and friend Julie Sale who took on the role of editor for this book. Her honesty, her eye for detail, and her warmth made writing this book an enjoyable and fun process. Julie is the director of the Contemporary Institute of Clinical Sexology (CICS), one of the UK and Europe's leading institutes in clinical sexology. My gratitude extends to the Institute for being so generous in allowing the use of their anatomy graphics in this book.

I would like to thank my current clinical supervisor, Dominic Davies, who is also the founder of Pink Therapy, an independent organisation dedicated to the populations of Gender, Sex and Relationship Diversities (GSRD). He continuously shares his extensive knowledge with me. I love that I never stop learning from him through our mutual passion for sexology. I would also like to thank my clinical supervisor, Judith C Turner, for her ongoing support and for making supervision a joyous and challenging experience.

I started my professional journey as a specialist in sex and relationship therapy with The London Diploma in Psychosexual and Relationship Therapy (LDPRT). I warmly thank the directors Judi Keshet-Orr and Bernd Leygraf for being leading teachers in the field. Throughout the years, I have been fortunate to learn from many influential specialists in the field of sexology and intimate relationships: Douglas Braun-Harvey, David Schnarch, Harville Hendrix, Helen LaKelly Hunt, and Esther Perel, to name a few. I have also been lucky to connect with many wonderful clinicians doing innovative work around the world, including Dr David Ley, Dr Nicole Prause, Cyndi Darnell, Babette Rothschild, Dr Joe Kort, Dr Markie Twist, Dr Francesca Tripoli, Dr Evie Kirana, Dr Filippo Nimbi, Dr Lori Beth Bisbey, and Dr Karen Gurney. I'm grateful for the ongoing support of colleagues and friends Kate Moyle, Dr Roberta Babb, Aoife Drury, Catriona Boffard, Remziye Kunelaki, Juliette Clancy, Lisa Etherson, Diana Moffat, Andrew Mirrlees, Julie Gaudion, David Piner, and Clare Staunton, as well as the wonderful CICS leadership team: Rima Hawkins, Lorraine McGinlay, Simon Wilson, and Kirstie McEwan. I thank you all so much.

I would like to send special thanks to Dr Angela Sharma who supported me with Chapter 5, checking for medical accuracy, as well as Dr Angela Wright for her encouragement and signposting of medical resources. I would like to thank my colleague Ronete Cohen for advising me on making the topic of disability a truly inclusive part of the conversations on sex and relationships. I would like to thank Dr Meg-John Barker for their ongoing support in keeping an inclusive language and their overall wisdom in sexology. Thank you to Nicholas Taylor for his excellent proofreading service.

I am grateful to all the wonderful sex therapists, sex coaches, and sex educators out there creating great content of accurate information on sex and relationships. There are too many to mention them all here, but I'd like to mention some of the trail blazers of sex-positivity: Franki Cookney, Lucy Rowett, Gigi Engle, Alix Fox, Paisley Gilmour, Topher Taylor, Lisa Welsh, and Samantha Evans.

Thank you to the College of Sexual and Relationship Therapy (COSRT) for being the UK's leading professional body for psychosexual and relationship therapists. I'm proud to be an accredited member.

Last, but not least, I would like to thank my husband, Dr James Rafferty, for his consistent love and support, and the joy he brings to my life.

GLOSSARY

Abstinence   the voluntary decision to abstain from sex, even if there is sexual desire.

Agender   not identifying with a gender. It may be described as "gender neutral" or "genderless".

Agoraphilia   being aroused by outdoor sex.

Agrexophilia   being aroused by having sex with the possibility to be overheard by others.

Amaurophilia   being aroused by having sex with someone who can't see them (using a blindfold, for example).

Anaclitism   being aroused by activities or objects associated with early childhood.

Anal Intercourse   the sexual practice of penis-in-rectum penetration.

Androphilia   being emotionally, sexually, and/or romantically attracted to masculinity.

Anilingus   (also known as rimming) the sexual practice of oral sex in the anal area, stimulating the anus with lips and tongue.

Asexuality   sexual orientation describing experiencing no sexual attraction but there may be a desire for a romantic relationship.

Autoerotic Asphyxiation   the sexual practice of self-strangulation while masturbating, with a hand or sex toy.

Autofellatio   the sexual practice of licking and sucking one's own penis.

Autosexuality   experiencing a sexual attraction towards themselves.

Barebacking   the sexual practice of having vaginal or anal intercourse without condoms.

BDSM   stands for bondage, discipline, submission, and sadomasochism. It is a group of sexual practices usually involving "power play", also known as "kink".

Bestiality   (also known as zoophilia) the act of sexually penetrating a living animal vaginally or anally by humans, or animals on humans. In England and Wales, it is a sexual offence.

Bicurious   people identifying as heterosexual who are interested in having a sexual or romantic experience with someone of the same gender.

Bigender   identifying as two genders. For example, male and female, or male and agender, or any other gender combination.

Bisexuality   sexual orientation describing the emotional, sexual, and/or romantic attraction to people of the same gender and different gender from their own.

Body Rubbing   (also known as dry humping or frottage) the sexual practice of rubbing bodies together, especially around the genital areas, fully clothed.

Candaulism   the sexual practice of watching a couple have sex.

Cisgender   the gender identity matches the sex assigned at birth.

CNM   stands for consensual non-monogamy (also called ENM: ethical non-monogamy) which are relationships that allow romantic and/or sexual contact with more than one person at a time.

Coitus   the sexual practice of penis-in-vagina penetration, also known as copulation or vaginal intercourse.

Coitus a mammilla   the sexual practice of stimulating the penis between a person's breasts, often to the point of ejaculation.

Compersion   the feeling of joy at seeing or hearing the sexual and/or romantic happiness that a partner has with other people.

Coprophilia   (also known as scat play or scatology) the sexual practice involving the use of human faeces.

Cuckolding   the sexual practice of being aroused by a partner having sex with someone else consensually. It is often related to the kink of Domination, submission, and humiliation.

Cunnilingus   the sexual practice of stimulating the vulva and the clitoris with oral sex using lips and tongue.

Cupiosexual   sexual orientation describing experiencing no sexual and/or romantic attraction but still desire to engage in sexual behaviours or have a sexual relationship.

Cybersex   the sexual practice of accessing sexual arousal and pleasure through online platforms, which includes masturbating with someone else on webcam, or watching/being watched masturbating.

Demisexual   sexual orientation describing feeling sexual attraction towards people with whom they have already established a strong emotional bond.

Digisexuality   sexual orientation describing the emotional, sexual, and/or romantic attraction to other people through devices and technology.

Dogging   the sexual practice of people enjoying couples (or other people) having sex in their car in a car park.

Erotic Massage   the sensual and sexual practice of a full body massage done by one or more people who are naked or partially naked, massaging the erogenous parts of the body and focusing on genitals for sexual pleasure until reaching an orgasm.

Exhibitionism   the sexual practice and arousal of being watched, either undressing, naked, in intimate and private spaces, having sex with other people or masturbating in front of others.

Felching   the sexual practice of licking semen out of the vagina or anus after intercourse that finished with ejaculation inside it.

Fellatio   the sexual practice of oral sex stimulating a penis, by licking or sucking with the lips, mouth, and tongue.

Fetishism   the sexual arousal in response to a specific object (shoes, food, silk, rubber, leather, etc.), a body part that is non-genital (breasts, feet, legs, armpits, hair, ears, etc.), or a practice (cross-dressing, role play, etc.).

Findom   means financial Domination, the kink of Dominant people demanding money from submissive people.

Fisting   the sexual practice of inserting a hand into the vagina or rectum of a sexual partner.

Foot fetish   (also known as podophilia) the sexual arousal of looking at, touching, or involving feet in the sexual practice.

Foreplay   the sexual practice in preparation for penetrative sex. For some people, "fore-play" is "main-play" or "core-play" as it's the part of sex that generates the most pleasure and orgasm.

Friends with benefits (FWB) friendships that allow an opportunity for sexual contact with each other, either occasionally or frequently.

Furries people who enjoy wearing animal costumes, usually colourful and cartoon character-like animals while having sex.

Gay sexual orientation describing the emotional, sexual, and/or romantic attraction to people of the same gender.

Gender fluid identifying with moving fluidly between genders with the identity shifting between male and female or neither.

Genderqueer identifying with being gender non-confirming, rejecting binary labels.

Gerontophilia the primary sexual attraction to the elderly.

Grayromantic experiencing romantic attraction rarely or not very strongly.

Graysexual experiencing sexual attraction either infrequently or not very intensely.

Group sex the sexual practice involving more than two partners at the same time. It is often known as an orgy.

Gynephilia the emotional, sexual, and/or romantic attraction to femininity.

Hebephilia the primary attraction to pubescent children.

Heteronormativity the assumption that heterosexuality is the only "normal" and everything else is "strange", "weird", or "abnormal".

Heterosexuality (also known as straight) sexual orientation describing the emotional, sexual, and/or romantic attraction to their binary opposite sex or a different gender from their own.

Hodophilia the arousal from travelling or when in a new and unfamiliar place.

Hotwifing the sexual practice of people sharing their very attractive wife with others for sexual pleasure. It is usually done within heterosexual relationships.

Incest sexual contact between close family-related people. It is illegal in England and Wales.

Intersex Biological diversity of chromosomes, genitals, gonads, hormones, additional reproductive anatomy.

Lesbian   sexual orientation describing women who have emotional, sexual, and/or romantic attraction towards other women.

Masturbation   the sexual practice of stimulating one's genitals with a hand, fingers, or masturbation toys.

Monogamish   a monogamous relationship that allows occasional intimate/sexual contacts with others.

Monogamy   a romantic and/or sexual relationship with one other person at any given time.

Mononormativity   the assumption that monogamy is the "gold standard", or the "normal" and everything else is "weird" or "abnormal".

Monosexuality   an emotional, sexual, and/or romantic attraction towards only one gender.

Multisexuality   an emotional, sexual, and/or romantic attraction to more than one gender.

Mummification   the sexual practice when one's entire body is wrapped, making the person unable to move. There is sometimes an agreement that the genitals, nipples, or anus are left exposed for sexual play while in mummification.

Necrophilia   the sexual practice of intercourse with a corpse. In England and Wales, the sexual penetration of a corpse is a sexual offence.

Omnisexuality   an emotional, sexual, and/or romantic attraction to people of all genders.

Paedophilia   the primary attraction to pre-pubescent children.

Pansexuality   an emotional, sexual, and/or romantic attraction to people regardless of their gender. Pansexual people are "gender blind".

Pegging   the sexual practice when a woman (usually cisgender) anally penetrates a man (usually cisgender) with fingers, sex toys, or using a strap-on.

Phone sex   having sexually explicit conversations with other people on the phone. It is usually accompanied by masturbation to the point of reaching an orgasm.

Polyamory   loving more than one person at any given time. Polyamory often includes sexual and romantic relationships with multiple partners but not always.

Polyandry   one woman married to multiple husbands.

Polyfidelity a closed group of people who are in CNM relationships with each other only; they all know each other and the introduction of strangers or new people in the system is forbidden. In the case of three people, it is also known as a throuple or *ménage à trois*.

Polygamy being married to multiple spouses. It is illegal in the UK.

Polygyny one man married to multiple wives.

Polysexuality an emotional, sexual, and/or romantic attraction to all genders.

Pomosexuality people who reject all labels that attempt to define sexuality and gender.

Pup play the kinky practice of dressing up as a dog, with a mask resembling a dog's face and the tail as a special butt plug. It is a practice predominantly popular with gay men in the leather fetish communities.

Queer people from the LGBTQ+ communities who reject heteronormativity.

Relationship Anarchy (RA) (also known as relationship queer) are relationships with the philosophy that each relationship is unique and equally important, whether sexual, romantic, or otherwise, and evolves organically into different dimensions.

Role play the sexual practice of acting out a fantasy, a story, or being a character that is different from everyday life.

Safer Sex the sexual practice of having sex in a way that prevents or limits the contraction of STIs.

Sapiosexuality an emotional, sexual, and/or romantic attraction to intelligence.

Shower the sexual practice of pouring some liquid over a partner for sexual arousal.

Sixty-nine the sexual practice of mutual oral sex with a partner at the same time.

Skoliosexual an emotional, sexual, and/or romantic attraction to people who are nonbinary, transgender, or genderqueer.

Swinging the sexual practice of couples (usually ones that identify themselves as monogamous) who occasionally engage in sexual activities with other couples or single people.

Teleiophilia the primary attraction to adults.

Third gender   not identify with either man or woman but identifies with another gender, called third gender.

Transgender   identifying as a gender that is different from the sex assigned at birth.

Upskirting   the offending practice of using a device (mirror or phone with extension equipment) to look under someone's skirt or dress without their consent. It is an offence under the Voyeurism Offences Act 2019.

Vanilla   the group of sex practices that are considered not kinky.

Voyeurism   the sexual practice of gaining sexual pleasure from watching others when they are naked or engaged in sexual activity.

V relationships   one person in a relationship with two different partners that are not in relationships with each other, thus creating a V-shaped relationship.

Watersports   (also known as urophilia or golden shower) the sexual practice of urinating on a partner, urinating on oneself, or watching someone else urinate.

INTRODUCTION

The last ten years have been an amazing time of growth for sexology. There have been many new interesting scientific studies conducted, helpful books published, more clinicians being drawn to the field, and more sex-positive conversations. There have been more people wanting specialist professional help to resolve sexual difficulties and their struggles in their relationships. Although there is so much more fantastic and accessible information about sex and relationships, there has also been an increase in misinformation on those topics. The demand for more content on sex and relationships created a tsunami of "products" and "programmes" soaked in myths and misinformation in order to monetise on the intimate struggles of people.

I decided to write this book because, over the years, I have become increasingly aware that people are being let down by misinformation. There has been a sharp increase in medical professionals, counsellors, and psychotherapists asking me to help them with their knowledge gap in sexology because their training/education did not cover it. When professionals are not trained in understanding the great diversity in gender, sexuality, and relationships, it allows too much room for assumptions and judgements.

I believe that the knowledge of contemporary sexology should not be reserved for professionals who work in healthcare. I think everybody should know more about it. In my experience, much of the distress that people feel about their sex lives and intimate relationships come from excruciatingly poor sex education. Unawareness in these areas become a fertile ground for myths to grow, causing greater problems in people's intimate lives.

DOI: 10.4324/9781003276913-1

This book is not about sex therapy; it is not a self-help book either. As the title says, it is a book about the basic knowledge of sexology, which means the contemporary knowledge of all aspects that relate to our sexuality and intimate relationships. I wrote this book in jargon-free language, hoping it can be a helpful reference point for professionals and laypeople in understanding themselves better, and filling the gap of poor sex education.

In Chapter 1, you will read about the history of sex and sexology, where it comes from, and how it developed to be what it is today. In Chapter 2, I will explain the diversities of gender and biological sex. In Chapter 3, I write about diverse sexual orientations. In Chapter 4, I focus on eroticism and fantasies. In Chapter 5, I offer a brief overview of the physiological aspects of sex because it's a crucial part of the overall field of sexology. In Chapter 6, I look at some of the various sexual practices that people engage in. In Chapter 7, I thought it was important to discuss pornography thoroughly as it is often a subject matter that is misunderstood, provoking much debate. In Chapter 8, I turn my attention to the different types of intimate relationships, which are an important part of sexology. I discuss love, too. Chapter 9 is about sexual offending. It is often an uncomfortable topic but crucial knowledge. Chapter 10, the last chapter, is dedicated to the relationship between sex, intimate relationships, and overall health. I aim to demonstrate how the knowledge of sexology plays a big part in our general well-being.

WORDS

In this book, you will read that words are important to me. Some people dislike labels and want to identify only as humans. For other people, words and labels are important because they can normalise experiences that are often unspoken in our society, thus reducing shame and a sense of defectiveness.

Words can also be a place of belonging and "home". They can be associated with a sense of "family of choice", peers, and being with people with a shared understanding of our specific culture, mindset, values, and philosophy.

Words can shape the way we think. Using the appropriate terms that are currently accepted can challenge prejudices and enhance inclusivity. Making an effort to use inclusive terms means that we help shape the collective mindset of our society.

Words can also help us be more curious about the immense diversity of humanity. You will read in this book that there isn't a single word or term that can describe accurately the vast diversity of being human. I endeavour to be as inclusive as possible while being aware that some of the words I use may not fit everybody. I want to assure my readers that my intentions and values of inclusivity are at the centre of my philosophy. As I make the commitment to embrace inclusivity, I also commit to continue to learn and adapt my language year after year to reflect our current understanding of diversity. This is why in this book you will read terms referring to gender, sexual orientations, and intimate relationships that are currently accepted, but these may change over time. The website Stonewall (stonewall. org.uk) keeps an updated glossary of accepted terms. I invite all of us to keep checking on a regular basis, as a commitment to inclusivity. If some words I use bring discomfort, I hope that, together, we can take this opportunity to continue the conversations of equality, diversity, and inclusivity.

I'm passionate about sexology because I believe it is a central part of what makes us human and alive, it helps us connect meaningfully with each other and the world around us. This book is my love letter to my profession of clinical sexology.

WHAT IS SEXOLOGY?

Sexology is the scientific study of human sexuality. The modern version of sexology recognises that the study of sexual behaviour cannot be separated from human intimate relationships because much of our sexual desire, arousal, pleasure, and behaviours occur in relation to the connection we have with ourselves and others in our intimate spaces. A person's psychosexual processes intertwine with their attachment patterns and desires. Therefore, sexology is more broadly the study of human sexuality and intimate relationships, which covers a wide range of subjects.

Some sexologists are academics and/or scientists, focusing on sexuality research and theories. Others focus on the clinical practice of sexology, aimed at helping people who struggle with their sex lives and relationships. Most clinical sexologists are psychotherapists or psychologists with an additional specialist training in clinical sexology (also known as psychosexual and relationship therapy, or sex therapy). The largest professional body governing clinical sexologists in the UK is the College of Sexual and Relationship Therapists (COSRT). In the USA, it is The American Association of Sexuality Educators, Counselors and Therapists (AASECT). Clinical sexologists who practise within the psychotherapeutic professions and who are members of such governing bodies practise talk-only therapy, which does not involve touching their clients. However, some also engage in embodied forms of therapy such as Somatic Experiencing or Sensorimotor Psychotherapy, where some consensual trauma-informed touch may occur. Some sexologists are trained in Sexological Bodywork, which can also extend to consensual intimate or erotic touch in an educational and/or healing capacity. Such Somatic Sex

DOI: 10.4324/9781003276913-2

Educators (SSE) may or may not have training in psychotherapy or similar professions. They work on a spectrum which can include talk, breath work, and touch-based approaches to sexual issues. They may be accredited by bodies like the Association of Certified Sexological Bodyworkers.

A BRIEF HISTORY OF SEX AND SEXUALITY

As far back as we can see, human beings have had a fascination with sex, sexual practices, and genitals. We have discovered cave paintings and ancient art featuring the depiction of men, women, and nonbinary people engaging in sexual activities with one or more people and showing a diverse range of sexual orientations. Since the beginning of humankind, various civilisations have used sexuality to make erotic art, to attain spirituality through sexual worship, and have incorporated sex into their daily lives. Over the centuries some civilisations and cultures have incorporated explicit sexuality as part of their societal acceptance and, at other times in history, it has been the opposite, with strong social prohibitions against the visibility of sex.

It might be hard for us to believe that there have been times and civilisations who embraced human sexuality in quite different, more explicit ways. Ancient art showing penises, vulvas, and diverse sexual activities are rampant throughout cultures and civilisations and they have been discovered all over the world. Those ancient erotic art forms were used to signpost a place as a "brothel" (or a place for sexual pleasure), to celebrate fertility, to tell sexual stories for entertainment, and even used as tombstones.

Here are some examples:

- A wine jug depicting a sex worker and a customer (dated between 480 and 470 BCE), Greece.
- A fresco in Pompeii depicting the rustic fertility god Priapus, who was also the protector of livestock and plants, often depicted with a permanent erection (dated between 89 BCE and 79 CE), Italy.
- A sculpture of a male sex organ (dated in the 6th millennium BCE), Ancient Anatolia, Turkey.

- A clay plaque depicting a couple having intercourse (dated 2nd millennium BCE, Old Babylonian Period), Mesopotamia (Iraq).
- A statue depicting sex, showing a disproportionately massive penis (dated Early Ptolemaic Period, 305–30 BCE), Alexandria, Egypt.
- An Etruscan amphora depicting sex between two men (dated 5th century BCE), Capua Vetere, Italy.
- Relief on one of the Khajuraho Group of Temples dedicated to both Hinduism and Jainism, depicting group sex (dated 11th century), Madhya Pradesh, India.
- A silver-gilt plate with the erotic scene of a threesome (dated 4th century BCE, Thracian Civilisation), Letnica, Bulgaria.
- An ancient sexual sculpture in the Dattatreya Temple (dated 15th century), Bhaktapur, Nepal.
- Ceramic depicting fellatio (dated 100 to 700 BCE by the Moche people), Peru.
- A jade erotic art piece made during the Ming Dynasty (1368–1644), China.
- A clay figurine of the fertility goddess (dated 7000–6100 BCE), Kermanshah, Iran.
- A painting of one man and two women stimulating each other's genitals (dated 1st century CE), Western Mexico.
- A Cherokee ceremonial stone pipe with a fellatio erotic scene (dated 10th century CE), Eastern Woodlands, Georgia, USA.
- Mother goddess, masturbating (dated 305–51 BCE, Ptolemaic Period), Egypt.

All these examples suggest that human beings have paid a lot of attention to sex and sexual activities, with an emphasis on the different meanings of sex: pleasure, procreation, and spirituality (or existentialism); but not always perceived as the "norm" in many cultures today.

In the UK, sexual prohibition and repression started in the Middle Ages with the Christian religion and continued through to the Victorian era. The 20th century saw major changes in our relationship with sex. There was a big movement in the 1960s and 70s of sexual liberation from the sex-negative Victorian era, lifting the taboo of sex and gaining more sexual freedom.

In England, the Sexual Offences Act was passed in 1967, which decriminalised homosexual acts between men aged over the age of

21. In 1994, the Criminal Justice and Public Order Act lowered the age of consent of gay men to 18, and in 2001, it was further lowered to 16. Meanwhile, the law was changed in Scotland in 1980 and in Northern Ireland in 1982. In 1973, the American Psychiatric Association (APA) removed the diagnosis of "homosexuality" as a mental disorder from the third edition of the Diagnostic manual (DSM-III) and the subsequent editions. Unfortunately, the sexual freedom of gay people was dampened again in the early 1980s with the HIV/AIDS epidemic. The global fear of the virus reinforced sexual prohibitions, largely led by religious movements, which used the opportunity of the virus to declare it a message of God against gay people. The sanctity of marriage between a man and a woman became stronger than ever, as well as the promotion of homophobia. The diagnosis of "homosexuality" remained a mental health disorder in the International Classification of Disease (ICD) by the World Health Organization (WHO) until 1990. It took even longer for transgender people to stop being unduly pathologised. The WHO declared that being transgender was no longer classified as a mental health disorder only in 2019.

Women also had to fight for their rights throughout history. The first feminist movement, the Suffragette movement, started in 1848, demanding a change for women's rights, which were sparse then. In the time of sexual liberation in the 1960s, the second wave of feminism took off, campaigning for sexual health rights, including reproductive rights, job opportunities, and speaking up about violence against women. Thanks to these movements, today, in the Western world, women have gained legal rights, yet, it is clear that our society is still largely patriarchal and misogynistic, judging by the number of assaults against women that still happen now. The modern discussions on misogyny and the safety of women (or lack thereof) were brought to the fore by the #MeToo movement in 2017. Today, in the 21st century, women are still fighting for equal pay or equal opportunities in decision-making roles, and to be taken as seriously as men. Women report that they still feel unsafe in the streets because the responsibility for safety is still placed on them ("don't go out alone at night", "don't wear a mini-skirt", "don't get drunk"), rather than on the perpetrators. In some other cultures, women's rights are almost non-existent, where they are still considered the property of the man and do not have basic rights such as education, the right to choose who to marry, or any access to sexual health. More recently, in 2022, the US Supreme Court overturned the legal right to abortion (referred to as Roe v Wade). It was a dark time in history that sharply brought to our awareness that the social justice we acquire may not last forever, and how women's rights are often under attack.

The modern Western views and ideas about sex and sexuality are still largely influenced by the echo of the prohibitions of religions, but there is also much more openness and accessibility to discuss sex and intimate relationships. This easier access to sexual content and information leaves many people in erotic conflicts, trying to navigate their learnt societal prohibitions (which may trigger shame) and their natural curiosity about sex.

Most religious spaces are notoriously forceful in prohibiting some sexual activities or even thoughts about those activities. I would argue that being so concerned about repressing sexuality also reflects a fascination with it. In our modern times, articles and books about sex are a "juicy" subject creating a lot of dividing opinions and strong moral judgements. For example, pornography is very popular, watched by millions of people, yet it is also perceived as dangerous. All of these indicate that our high interest with sex continues.

When I visited the Sex Machines Museum in Prague, it was fascinating to see how much energy human beings put into technologies for the sole purpose of sexual pleasure. The museum displayed a *godemiche*, a French invention that is the ancestor of our modern dildo. It is phallus-shaped, made of bone or ivory, and for the purpose of sexual pleasure for people with vulvas. It had an apparatus where the user could place a photograph of their lover so that they could watch the photograph during masturbation. When the lover changed, they could simply change the photograph. There was also the "magic box", a large carriage with small windows all around it. Inside would lie a partially dressed woman and people would pay money to peer into the windows and watch the woman. This "magic box" was used during market days or in rural festivities. It was the early version of what we now call the "peep show".

There were also other artefacts that represented times in history of religious prohibition. For example, in the 1700s, a cagoule nightie, which has its origins in France, was a long shirt that people would wear with a split at the genital level that allowed intercourse without bodies touching in "sinful ways". Some of those shirts had the embroidered words *Dieu Le Veut* (God wants it like this) on them. Also in France, it was customary in the early 20th century to gift a newlywed woman a porcelain chamber pot with the inscriptions *A la mariee* (to the bride). The chamber pot was painted with an eye on the bottom, which represented both the greedy and guarding eye of the husband and reflected a time when a wife was regarded as the sexual property of the husband and the infidelity of the wife was the biggest sin.

In the year 1450, it was usual to wear pubic wigs. Back then, women would shave their pubic hair for hygiene in order to avoid pubic lice, so instead, they wore a pubic wig. How time has changed! The museum also displayed gazillions of ancient dildos, some in the shape of a hand or fingers, others being more creative, including a plastic penis attached to a teddy bear (for those who like a bit of fur), and some objects that are the precursors of what we now commonly find in specialist BDSM sex shops, like leather masks, handcuffs, spikes, oxygen control devices, and so on.

Wherever we look in history, either through art or objects used in the past, sex and sexuality have always been an important and fascinating part of people's lives, in terms of carnal pleasure, human desires, excitement, and aliveness, as well as prohibitions and the attempts to either counter them or comply with them.

Much of our best-loved human stories, from the Greek tragedies, religious texts, and Shakespeare, to our more modern stories in films and television series, have strong themes of sex, betrayal (or loyalty), attachments, romantic love, and human connections. Indeed, these sexological themes are central to our human heart, how we gain a sense of ourselves, and how we perceive the world around us. These are the very core parts that hold some of the most meaningful treasures of our experiences of being alive.

A BRIEF HISTORY OF SEXOLOGY

The term "sexology" was coined by the American phrenologist Orson Squire Fowler in 1852 (Kahan, 2021). It was made popular by Elizabeth Osgood Goodrich Willard, with her publication *Sexology as the Philosophy of Life: Implying Social Organization and Government* (1867).

The interest in theorising sexual behaviours in a scientific framework grew in the 19th century with the publication of *Psychopathia*

Sexualis (1886) by Richard Freiherr von Krafft-Ebing, which was mostly concerned with classifying (and pathologising) sexual behaviours. Nevertheless, it is thought to be the first scientific text of sexology.

In England, the scientific field of sexology was born in 1897, with Havelock Ellis who challenged pathologising same-gender sexual behaviours, which was revolutionary in his time. His seminal publication *Sexual Inversion* was the first non-pathological study of "homosexuality" published in Britain.

The first scholarly journal, *Journal of Sexology*, edited by Magnus Hirschfeld, appeared in 1908 with prominent clinicians of the time contributing to its articles. Thanks to Havelock Ellis's publications, The British Society for the Study of Sex Psychology was founded in 1913, with the particular agenda to advance sex reform.

Sigmund Freud, the founder of psychoanalysis, was one of the main influential clinicians in the field of sexology between the late 19th century and the early 20th century, particularly with his famous theory of sexual development from infancy to adulthood with the five psychosexual stages: oral, anal, phallic, latent, and genital. Much of Freud's theories have been criticised since; however, his texts are well-respected and are still a reference point for psychodynamic and psychoanalytic schools of therapy.

In Britain, the Victorian era was reductive in thinking about sexuality. Germany, however, became the leading country for sexology, led by the aforementioned physician Magnus Hirschfeld who advocated for gay and transgender rights. He established the first gay rights organisation in the world in 1897. He also founded the world's first sexology institute, the Institute for Sexual Science, in Berlin in 1919, which held a vast library and archives on sexology studies. He was a pioneer in understanding the spectrum of gender and sexuality diversities. Sadly, the institute and its rich library were destroyed when the Nazis came to power.

After the Second World War, sexology was reborn, with a new generation of scientists in the United States and Europe undertaking studies on human sexuality. Alfred Kinsey, an American biologist, Professor of Entomology and Zoology, and sexologist, founded the Institute for Sex Research in 1947, which is now known as the Kinsey Institute at Indiana University. He published *Sexual Behavior in the Human Male* in 1948, which became very popular, reaching the New York Times bestseller list. Alfred Kinsey made sexology a popular topic and a public discourse. Following the success of that publication, he then published *Sexual Behavior in the Human Female* in 1953. The books were called the "Kinsey Reports" by the media. In those books, Kinsey featured his scale, identifying the spectrum of sexual orientations, with "heterosexual" at one end and "homosexual" at the other. This is now known as "The Kinsey Scale".

John Money was another prominent physician known for his contribution to psychoendocrinology and developmental sexology. He founded the Gender Identity Clinic at Johns Hopkins University in 1966 and developed gender-affirming treatment protocols. He coined the term "gender role" and later refined it to "gender-identity/role".

Kurt Freund, a Czech Canadian physician was a pioneer in human sexual arousal in the 1950s. He developed phallometry and created an instrument measuring sexual arousal in men. His theories contributed to the removal of "homosexuality" as a psychiatric disorder in the American Psychiatric Association listings. Freund was best known for his studies on paedophiles. He was one of the first physicians to speak about sexual orientations being set during one's development and that any attempts to change someone's sexuality is futile. Instead, he proposed to focus the treatment of paedophiles and sex offenders on teaching them impulse control to prevent sexual offending.

William Masters and Virginia Johnson were the clinicians who developed our understanding of sexual response and were the pioneers of the treatment of sexual dysfunctions, which was the starting point for our modern field of psychosexual therapy (also known as sex therapy). Their books, *Human Sexual Response* (1966) and *Human Sexual Inadequacy* (1970), were great successes. They became famous for their four-stage model of sexual response: (1) Excitement, (2) Plateau, (3) Orgasm, and (4) Resolution. They founded the Reproductive Biology Research Foundation in 1978, which was later renamed the Masters and Johnson Institute.

The epidemic of HIV/AIDS in the early 1980s created a sudden change in the direction of the research in sexology, focusing efforts on understanding the virus. Sadly, it was also a time when sex-negative narratives resurged. People became terrified of sex, especially multiple-partnered sex, further promoting the Christian virtues of abstinence and monogamous marriage. It was also the time when promiscuity was framed under the conceptualisation of "sex addiction", which was used as a medicalised term to promote monogamy. In the 21st century, "sex addiction" is still a strong narrative although most of the worldwide scientific community now refute the term because of lack of clinical evidence (APA, DSM-5, 2013).

It seems that, over the decades, the field of sexology was largely advanced by the clinicians who were passionate about social justice and challenged the thinking of their time, related to gender, sexuality, and relationship diversities. Science was not the only discipline that helped the development of sexology. Intellectuals and thinkers were also important in the discourse of gender, sexuality, and relationships. Philosopher Michel Foucault published three volumes of *The History of Sexuality: The Will to Knowledge* (volume one in 1976, and volumes two and three, *The Use of Pleasure* (1984a) and *The Care of The Self* (1984b). A fourth volume was completed just before he died but locked away in a vault for three decades, *Confessions of the Flesh* (2021). Foucault made a significant contribution in rethinking the common assumptions about sex.

THE BIO-PSYCHO-SOCIAL MODEL

The widely accepted contemporary lens in which to conceptualise people's sexual behaviours and functioning, and gender expression is the bio-psycho-social model. It was first established by George L. Engel and Jon Romano of the University of Rochester (n.d.). This model allows clinical sexologists to understand people's experiential sense of self through a framework that takes into account the complex intertwining relationships between their biology, psychology, and the social world around them.

> *Biological factors* include the sex we are assigned at birth, our inherited genetics, the way our brain works, and the strengths and limitations of our body.
>
> *Psychological factors* include our moods in the here and now, our personal experiences in childhood and onwards, and the lessons – or stories about ourselves – we have learnt from those experiences. It also includes our values, our self-reflection, and our attachment styles.

Social factors include the cultural messages we get both in the here and now and those of childhood (there could be various conflicting cultural messages), family "rules", pressure to conform to heteronormativity (the assumption that being heterosexual is the only "normal" and everything else is "strange"), life circumstances, financial health, social class, particular status or positions, and religious messages.

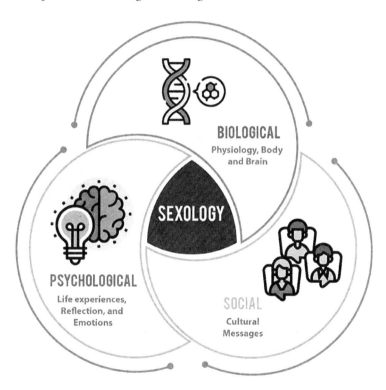

Figure 1.1 The BioPsychoSocial Model

WHY IS SEXOLOGY IMPORTANT?

As you can see from its history, the field of sexology was, and still is, at the forefront of advancing contemporary thinking and clinical understanding of sexual desire, arousal, and behaviours, pushing the boundaries of taboo and challenging pre-conceived ideas and myths about gender, sexuality, and relationship diversities.

The field of sexology contributes to the fundamental acceptance of the human right of freedom to sexual pleasure and the autonomy to conduct our intimate relationships as we choose, as well as challenging the misinformation and reducing the shame of diverse normative human sexual behaviours.

The digital age of the 21st century has created an illusion of being the time of information, but, unfortunately, with topics related to sex and relationships, it seems that it is the age of misinformation and pseudo-science. People tend to mistake opinions with facts. Many people live in the echo chamber of their carefully curated social media. They've lost the art of checking sources of information landing in their social media feed. It seems impossible to agree to disagree, or to hold different "truths" and different opinions. Some brilliant sexologists and sex educators consistently get blocked by some technology algorithm for sharing helpful and appropriate information about sex and relationships on social media, while many damaging myths continue to thrive unchallenged on those platforms.

It is common for clinical sexologists to meet clients/patients who become distressed about their sex lives and relationships because they think:

- Their vulva doesn't look right.
- Their penis isn't big enough.
- They worry something is drastically wrong because they have more sexual desire than their partner's.
- Sex is unsatisfying because they don't orgasm at the same time as their partner.
- They think their partner doesn't fancy them because they masturbate to pornography.
- They think their partner should meet all of their needs.
- They think their partner should know what they're feeling without being told.
- They are unhappy with their sex lives because they think sex should be spontaneous and should happen daily or weekly.
- They are disappointed because they thought that having a baby would be easy, full of joy, and would make their partner more caring.

- They think something's wrong with them because they have a specific fetish that turns them on a lot.

The list goes on. All of these distresses are made from shame, anger, resentment, sadness, and disappointment induced by public misinformation on sex and relationships. This is one of the reasons why the field of sexology is so important. It is the main discipline that can meaningfully help individuals, couples, and those in multi-partnered relationships resolve their problems and thrive.

For many people, the cause of distress is feeling bad about themselves because they think they are "broken" or "wrong" if their sexual attraction doesn't fit with what society is prescribing as "normal"

1. Marie, a heterosexual cisgender woman (cisgender means her gender identity matches the one assigned at birth) loves sex. She enjoys having sex with multiple partners, one at a time and on different days. She has good relationships with these men, feels completely fulfilled with her sex life, and feels safe with all her sexual partners because there is mutual respect and consent. She loves living on her own and she doesn't want to have children. She feels shamed on a regular basis by colleagues and her family of origin, telling her that something must be wrong with her for not wanting to "settle down" and be a mother. She has been called a "slut" several times by members of her family. The root of her distress is not her sex life but the judgements of others.

2. Joe is a heterosexual cisgender man who loves pegging, which is the sexual practice of being anally penetrated. He has the best time sexually and the best orgasms with pegging. He is successful on dates and he is generally able to find sexual partners whom he can do pegging with, but after a while, those sexual partners want to stop doing it and prefer to do "the normal stuff". He has often been told by the women he dates, and some friends with whom he was courageous enough to share his sexual preference, that there must be something wrong with him for loving being penetrated more than doing the penetration. Some have suggested to him that he must be a "repressed gay man", while others have laughed at him. Joe's sexual preference is completely normative, yet he feels damaged because of other people's judgements.

The psychotherapy and psychology professions aren't without their own problems. Some topics are hotly debated in an attempt to become more inclusive and sex positive. Typically, core training in psychotherapy and psychology does not include any (or hardly any) knowledge on how to work with sexual problems, or with the diverse populations of lesbian, gay, bisexual, trans people (LGBTQ+), and asexual, pansexual people, and so on. The psychotherapy and psychology fields are criticised for being largely a white, heterosexual, middle-class and ableist profession, and for teaching students to only treat this very population, rather than paying attention to the great range of human diversities. It is slowly changing but there is much room for improvement.

Clinicians who misunderstand sexual orientations and gender identities might believe that heterosexuality is the only "normal" and the rest is a pathology that can be cured. The second version of the Memorandum of Understanding on Conversion Therapy in the UK (2017) indicates that attempting to change someone's sexual orientation or gender identity is unethical and should not be promoted nor practised in the UK because it causes great harm. The document has been signed by all major psychotherapy and psychology professional regulating bodies. It is the pledge to make therapy safer for LGBTQ+ people.

The field of contemporary sexology helps with offering accurate specialist information on gender, sexuality, and relationships in order to avoid people being psychologically (and sometimes physically) harmed and shamed by others, including professionals.

SEX-POSITIVITY

Sex-positivity seems to have become a buzzword, but it is also misunderstood. Sex-positivity doesn't mean "anything goes", and it is not a "woke" term for saying "peace and love". Sex-positivity is best described as being authentic with our sexuality, gender expression, intimate relationships, and making conscious choices based on the wisdom of awareness. Sex-positivity relies on the thorough knowledge of ourselves so that we can be clear about boundaries and consent. Apart from the boundaries that are drawn by the law, the rest is subjective and up to each of us to draw for ourselves, making sure that explicit consent conversations match them. Therefore, each of us can have our own definition of sex-positivity. Mine are:

1. Exploring, embracing, and celebrating people's sexual fantasies, thoughts, desires, arousals, and behaviours, what I call their "Erotic Template" (see Chapter 4), without judgement.
2. Accepting that one person's erotic turn-on can be another person's erotic turn-off.
3. Being loyal to sexual authenticity: being aware of our erotic processes and keeping in touch with it as it changes over time, with new experiences and maturing.
4. Understanding sexual boundaries. What is legal and consensual? What feels good and what doesn't feel good.
5. Understanding that sex and love are not addictive. There are also no such things as "sexual anorexia" or "love anorexia".
6. Understanding, accepting and celebrating the wide range of gender identities and expressions, sexual orientations, and diverse forms of relationships, including transgender people, asexuality, bisexuality, queer, kinks, fetishes, polyamory, etc.
7. Being willing to learn more about gender, sex and relationship diversities when we think we have a blind spot.
8. Understanding that gender expression, sexual behaviours, and relationship settings need to align with a person's core values, integrity, and natural orientations.
9. Accepting and celebrating all body shapes.
10. Being willing to challenge sex-negativity and to promote sex-positivity, pleasure-positivity, and gender, sex, and relationship diversities with our peers and communities.

(Adapted from my book: *Compulsive Sexual Behaviours, a Psycho-sexual Treatment Guide for Clinicians*, Neves, 2021)

As you can see, an important feature of sex-positivity and sexology is to understand sexual freedom and sexual pleasure as human rights. The World Association for Sexual Health (WAS) made a declaration on sexual pleasure (2019):

Sexual pleasure should be exercised within the context of sexual rights, particularly the rights to equality and non-discrimination, autonomy and bodily integrity, the right to the highest attainable standard of health and freedom of expression.

Dr Neff (2020) describes the sex-positive movement as:

> a social, political and philosophical movement that promotes and embraces sexuality and sexual expression, with an emphasis on safe and consensual sex. Sex positive relationships are ones where partners support each other's choices and decisions without judgement, guilt or slut shaming. In a sex positive relationship, you can be whoever you want sexually, and do whatever you want sexually, without having to apologize for your sexual identity or expression, so long as you are not causing real harm to anyone else. In a sex positive relationship, you have permission to love your whole sexual body unconditionally, right now. Being sex positive can be best understood as a reaction to outdated misogynistic, patriarchal and religious structures that have sought to confine and control people's sexuality for far too long, and that crucially no longer serve us.
>
> (2020, p. 9)

SEXOLOGY AND DISABILITY

I confess that sexology does not escape ableism, as much as what is written and researched is through the lens of those who are not disabled. Disabled people are often infantilised (perceived as immature people who are incapable of making rational decisions) and desexualised (perceived as sexually undesirable or assuming they can't consent to sex and therefore forbidding them from having sex). Disabled people have sexual needs, like most people. Non-disabled people make a lot of assumptions about disabled people's sex lives without actually asking them. Some people with mental health difficulties and learning disabilities know what they want sexually and are able to express it, but the non-disabled population might not listen to them. There is an opportunity for the sexology field to extend its social justice of the human rights of people's freedom to sexual pleasure and autonomy to disabled people. They must not be excluded from the conversations about sex and intimate relationships.

The Equality Act 2010 in England, Wales and Scotland define a person as having a disability if:

(a) The person has a physical or mental impairment, and
(b) The impairment has a substantial and long-term adverse effect on the person's ability to carry out normal day-to-day activities.

There are various types of disabilities that can cause issues with sex and relationships, some of the most common ones are (but are not limited to):

• Physical disabilities (physical impairments such as upper limb disability, lower limb disability, and manual dexterity).
• Visual impairment and blindness.
• Hearing impairment and deafness.
• Speech and language disabilities.
• Cognitive or learning disabilities.
• Mental health or psychiatric disabilities.
• Organic brain disorders as a result of diseases or injury to the brain (such as Alzheimer's disease, stroke, or dementia).

Some physical conditions are progressive, which means they get worse over time but can fluctuate, such as:

• Multiple sclerosis (neurological deterioration)
• Muscular dystrophy (muscular disorders)
• Chronic arthritis (inflammation of the joints)

Some physical conditions are non-progressive (remaining stable):

• Cerebral palsy (a neurological condition)
• Spina bifida (a congenital malformation of the spinal cord)
• Spinal cord injury (neurological damage resulting from a severe accident)

There are some non-progressive physical conditions that can fluctuate:

• Fibromyalgia – chronic pain condition
• Chronic fatigue syndrome – chronic fatigue condition

You will notice that much of the language that we use regarding disabled people is through a medicalised lens of "impairment" in the context of our Western definition of "normal" and "functioning", which may be problematic and a further block to understanding their lived experiences.

The television series *Special*, created by Ryan O'Connell which premiered in 2019, featuring a main character with cerebral palsy (played by Ryan O'Connell, too) highlights the sexual and romantic needs of disabled people. This television show invited its audience to fall in love with a disabled character.

There are different types of mental health conditions that may disrupt sexual functioning and intimate relationships. For example, depression has an effect on sexual desire and sexual functioning, but so do anti-depressant medications. Anorexia can have a negative effect on sexual functioning, too. In my practice, I see numerous people with complex post-traumatic stress disorder (C-PSTD), which causes serious disruptions in people's sexual functioning, their attachment styles and their intimate relationships, especially if one of their post-traumatic symptoms is dissociation (disconnecting from thoughts, feelings, memories, or their sense of identity).

Some disabilities are visible, but some are invisible. People who have invisible disabilities (mental health problems, chronic fatigue, or people with endometriosis or fibromyalgia, to name only a few) can often be dismissed or even attacked when they ask for help for their "invisible" needs. Consistent body pain, fatigue, and the everyday stress of navigating a world made for non-disabled people will have an impact on an individual's sex life and their relationships.

The best way to navigate sex and relationships when disability is a factor is to step back from an ableist perspective and work to understand the impact of the individual's specific needs. If you are a clinician, it is imperative that you don't avoid questions about your disabled patients' sex lives because they do have an erotic mind and a body with erogenous zones.

There are people who are neurodiverse, and, as the modern term suggests, this isn't considered a disability any longer but a diversity of brain structures that creates different ways to perceive the world. For example, autism is best thought of as an identity rather than a disability. Of course, neurodiversity will also have an impact on sex and relationships as communication and sensory responses may well be experienced differently.

INTERSECTIONALITY

Human beings are complex because we live within multiple intersections of identities, and meanings, some of which are our own meanings and some within the context of our culture and the environment we live in. Typically, the awareness of our relational and sexual selves will be influenced by those multitudes of intersections.

1. Aysha is a cisgender woman who was born in the UK. She's from a Pakistani family who have strong Islamic views on the role of women. Although she is independent here in the UK, she has varying ways of identifying herself and connecting with the different parts of her intersectionality. In her work as a lecturer in a university, one of her defining features is religious faith because she wears her headscarf and she's aware that most people see this first. The second feature is her intellectual authority, which positions her in her third feature as a middle-class person. When she's with her family of origin, her first defining feature changes to being a woman, which means a provider of nurture for the rest of her family. Her intellect and social position do not matter, only what she can do for the men in her family matters. She's also aware that her brothers have different rights and statuses in her family of origin. In her independent life, she can connect with being assertive with her sexual needs and sexual pleasure, feeling men are her equal and she can voice explicit consent as to what she expects from them. When she's with her family of origin, she connects in conversations only about her plans to become a wife and a mother someday, and she does not divulge dating multiple men.

2. Pete is a cisgender gay man from Poland living in London. In Poland, his name is Piotr, but in the UK he prefers to be called Pete because English-speaking people tend to have difficulties in pronouncing his name. He doesn't want to make them uncomfortable. In the UK, he fully connects with his sexual orientation and he's happy in a gay monogamous relationship. Back in Poland,

he does not connect with his sexuality at all for his own safety, as the current government is homophobic, and so are his parents. Pete is filled with sadness about that. However, in Poland, he can connect with being a successful man and being the provider for his family of origin. In Poland, he is perceived as a businessman; in the UK, he prefers to be seen as a desirable gay man.

3. Steven is a cisgender heterosexual man. He is now in his 40s and he is not interested in a monogamous relationship. He enjoys BDSM and going to sex parties. He has a good network of BDSM friends and feels fulfilled. At work, he is considered to be mysterious and "always single". Some people perceive him as a "dark horse" while others wonder if he's not interested in sex because he's not married. At work, Steven wears a suit and he connects with his professional self. But it is not until he wears his leather gear that he connects with a totally different part of himself, his erotic self, which he firmly separates from work.

Intersectionality and the bio-psycho-social model can help us understand that there are many facets to human beings and, when we meet someone, we might only see one part of their identity. This is why it is so important not to make quick assumptions in our perception of others, we hardly ever see all the dimensions of one person. We don't truly know what another person is going through, thinking, or feeling because it is actually impossible to fully know it unless this person lets you into all of their intersecting identities. A psychotherapist, or clinical sexologist, is usually one of the rare people who have the immense privilege to be invited into the various aspects of a person.

Sexology can help everyone make better sense of their human experiences in their connection with themselves and others. Fulfilling sex lives and intimate relationships are the pulsing heart of the vast web of complex intersections that make people human, and feeling alive.

SUMMARY

Sex and intimate relationships fascinate people. From the very beginning of humankind, sex and intimate relationships have been a focus of our existence, a crucial ingredient for survival. It is no wonder these have taken centre stage in the interests of human beings. The field of sexology was born out of these interests, but sexologists brought a scientific lens to their curiosity, trying to understand human sexual desire, arousal, and behaviours more objectively. The field of sexology has often reacted against the sexual and relationship prohibitions of the time, which were the motivations for advancing the field further. Those motivations were largely to challenge society's views of gender, sexuality, and relationship diversities. We have come a long way in terms of acceptance and sex-positivity, but there is still much to do because the digital age brings as much misinformation as it does accurate information. It is easy to be confused about sex and relationships. Ultimately, the field of sexology goes far beyond what people do in the bedroom and with whom. It helps us be more accepting of each other. Disabled people, neurodiverse people, LGBTQ+ people, people of all racial identities and cultures are welcome because difference is a core feature of diversity and can help us understand one of the most fundamental questions we grapple with – what it means to be human.

Reflective questions:

1 What was your sex education like?

2 What have you learnt about gender, sex, and relationships that you consider "normal"?

3 When do you notice that you come up with a judgement in relation to people's gender, sex, and relationships?

4 What are the things you find "weird"?

5 Do you know why you find those things "weird"?

6 Are you aware of the source of some of your preconceptions and assumptions about gender, sex, and relationships?

7 What are the topics within the areas of gender, sex, and relationships that you are curious about and want to learn more about, and those topics you don't want to know more about?

FURTHER READING

The Sex Myth. Why Everything We're Told Is Wrong, by Dr Brooke Magnanti (2012).

The Psychology of Human Sexuality (Second Edition), by Justin J. Lehmiller (2018).

Sex Positive. Redefining our Attitudes to Love and Sex, by Dr Kelly Neff (2020).

REFERENCES

American Psychiatric Association (2013). *Diagnostic and Statistical Manual of Mental Health Disorders*, Fifth Edition (DSM-5). American Psychiatric Publishing. Arlington, VA.

Ellis, H. (1897). *Sexual Inversion*. Reprinted in 2018 by Createspace Independent Publishing Platform, Adeptio (Unforgettable Classic Series). Philadelphia.

Equality Act 2010 (2010). [Available Online]: https://www.legislation.gov.uk/ukpga/2010/15/section/6?view=extent

Foucault, M. (1976). *The History of Sexuality: Volume One, The Will to Knowledge*. Penguin Books Ltd. London.

Foucault, M. (1984a). *The History of Sexuality: Volume Two, The Use of Pleasure*. Penguin Books Ltd. London.

Foucault, M. (1984b). *The History of Sexuality: Volume Three, The Care of the Self*. Penguin Books Ltd. London.

Foucault, M. (2021). *The History of Sexuality: Volume Four, Confessions of the Flesh*. Penguin Classics. London.

Kahan, B. (2021). The Unexpected American Origins of Sexology and Sexual Science: Elizabeth Osgood Goodrich Willard, Orson Squire Fowler, and the Scientification of Sex. *History of the Human Sciences*, 34(1), 71–88. doi:10.1177/0952695120910051

Kinsey, A., Pomeroy, W.B., & Martin, C.E. (1948). *Sexual Behavior in the Human Male*. Saunders. Philadelphia.

Kinsey, A., Pomeroy, W.B., Martin, C.E., & Gebhard, P. (1953). *Sexual Behavior in the Human Female*. Saunders. Philadelphia.

Masters, W.H., & Johnson, V.E. (1966). *Human Sexual Response*. Bantam Books. Toronto; New York.

Masters, W.H., & Johnson, V.E. (1970). *Human Sexual Inadequacy.* Bantam Books. Toronto; New York.

Memorandum of Understanding on Conversion Therapy in the UK, Version 2 (2017, October) [Available Online]: https://www.cosrt.org.uk/wp-content/uploads/2019/08/MoU2-Revision-3-7-19.pdf

Neff, K. (2020). Sex Positive. Redefining our Attitudes to Love and Sex. Watkins Media Limited. London.

Neves, S. (2021). *Compulsive Sexual Behaviours. A Psycho-Sexual Treatment Guide for Clinicians.* Routledge. Abingdon, Oxon.

Osgood Goodrich Willard, E. (1867). *Sexology as the Philosophy of Life: Implying Social Organization and Government.* JR. Walsh. Chicago, Ill. [Available online]: https://wellcomecollection.org/works/meujcs8r/items?canvas=1

Special (2019). Television Series Created by Ryan O'Connell. *Netflix.*

University of Rochester. (n.d.). The Biopsychosocial Model. [Available Online]: https://www.urmc.rochester.edu/medialibraries/urmcmedia/education/md/documents/biopsychosocial-model-approach.pdf. Accessed: 13 August 2022.

Von Krafft-Ebing, R. (1886). *Psychopathia Sexualis.* Reprinted in 2011, Arcade Publishing. New York.

SEX AND GENDER

The topic of gender and sex is often intensely charged with emotions as these conversations are complex and multi-dimensional. They take into account different disciplines and different schools of thought: political, moral, medical, psychological, and philosophical. It is easy to be confused about the subject if we observe this matter from one window and not another. In this chapter, I'm going to attempt to bring some clarity to the subject, according to our most contemporary understanding.

THE DIFFERENCE BETWEEN SEX AND GENDER

Sex is a biological identifier connected to the anatomy we are born with. Male and female are sex identifiers assigned to us at birth in line with the appearance of our genitals. Gender is self-identified and socially constructed. The words man, woman, and nonbinary are gender terms.

The sexologist John Money was one of the first clinicians to introduce the terminology distinguishing sex and gender. The distinction was made because some people's gender expression did not match the sex they were assigned at birth (for an easy and helpful explanation about sex and gender, I recommend looking at the free resource called *The Genderbread Person*: genderbread.org).

The UK Office for National Statistics (2019) offer their definition of sex and gender:

DOI: 10.4324/9781003276913-3

"The UK government defines sex as:

- referring to the biological aspects of an individual as determined by their anatomy, which is produced by their chromosomes, hormones and their interactions.
- generally male or female.
- something that is assigned at birth."

The UK government defines gender as:

1. "a social construction relating to behaviours and attributes based on labels of masculinity and femininity; gender identity is a personal, internal perception of oneself and so the gender category someone identifies with may not match the sex they were assigned at birth.
2. where an individual may see themselves as a man, a woman, as having no gender, or as having a nonbinary gender – where people identify as somewhere on a spectrum between man and woman."

The normal differentiation of sex is observed in three aspects:

1. *Genetic or chromosomal*: sex chromosomes are typically XX (female) and XY (male).
2. *Gonadal differentiation*: the development of ovaries or testes.
3. *Phenotypes*: the appearance of the external genitalia and the secondary sexual characteristics that develop at puberty (which requires functioning hormones and hormone receptors).

Sex development occurs between week 8 to week 16 of pregnancy. Sometimes mutual congruence of the genetic, gonadal, and phenotype does not exist which can create variations of sexual differentiation.

The determination of sex is done by karyotyping, which means looking at gonadal and genital sexual characteristics. In the UK, birth certificates are still binary "M" or "F" and must be filed within 42 days after birth (21 days in Scotland). Other countries, like Germany for example, are legally recognising intersex people.

Many people think that sex and gender are binary, a belief that there are only two distinct biological sexes (male and female) and two genders (man and woman). Dr Debra Soh (2020) is one of the neuroscientists and clinicians asserting unequivocally that biological sex is binary because it is measured on gametes (sperm for men and eggs for women) and there are no variations in those. However, many scientists in the fields of biology, endocrinology, genetics, neuroscience, and reproductive science disagree with the binary thinking. The understanding that biological sex exists on a spectrum is now well established; the proof is that intersex people exist.

The chromosomal sex comprises of 23 pairs, usually including an X from the mother, and an X or Y from the father. Usually, the typical female karyotype is 46, XX and the male is 46, XY, but other variations exist such as: 45, X and 47, XXY; or combinations of 45, X/46, XY or 46, XX/46, XY (dsdfamilies, 2019). Within that spectrum the number of biological combinations is boundless. Even on a chromosome level, it seems that there is a lot of diversity, and not binary.

Gender is not binary because it is self-identified and it is a social construct. There is also a wide spectrum between feeling like a man or woman, including agender (neither man nor woman). For those of us whose sex assigned at birth matches how we feel inside, it might be very hard to grasp the subtleties and difficulties of those who do not have the same experience. In fact, I think it is impossible to know what it feels like if we do not experience it. However, I believe that not understanding doesn't mean we can't accept the diversity of gender identities. It is impossible for a cisgender man to understand what it feels like to be pregnant, yet they can happily live side-by-side with pregnant people and acknowledge their presence in the world. Perhaps we can do the same with nonbinary and transgender people. Being on a gender spectrum is not a new concept, it has always existed and is embraced in many cultures around the world.

1. *Fa'afafines and Fa'afatamas in Samoa*
   In Samoan culture, the people who are assigned male at birth and identify as women are called "Fa'afafines". The people who are assigned female at birth and identify as men are called "Fa'afatamas". They are fully accepted in that culture as a fluid gender that is as equally valid as cisgender men and women.

2. *Two-Spirit in Navajo culture*
   In the Navajo culture, "Two-Spirit" are people who identify with embodying both the spirits of masculinity and femininity. The "Two-Spirit" people have an important status in that culture as a channel between the physical and spiritual worlds.

3. *Sekrata in Madagascar*
   In Madagascar, the third gender called "Sekrata" is well recognised as part of their communities.

4. *Hijras in South Asia*
   Hijras are third gender people who are associated with sacred powers. They have their own ancient language and culture where there are no boundaries to gender expressions.

5. *Metis in Nepal*
   Nepal officially recognises the third gender as a legitimate legal status. Metis describes people who are assigned male at birth and identify as women.

The idea of binary gender became the dominant narrative in our Western culture with colonialism, which came with the Christian faith. Alex Iantaffi (2021) eloquently writes:

> Post-Christian interpretations of history have permeated the collective imagination through books, movies, documentaries and poetry to the point that we have needed to actively re-imagine and re-member people outside of a cisgender binary of male/female back into a history of which they were already part.
>
> (2021, p. 25)

Moreover, in Western countries, it is only in the 20th century that we associated specific colours with specific genders for babies (pink for girls, blue for boys). Before then, babies were mostly all dressed in white dresses, regardless of their sex assigned at birth. It is thought that the colour association of specific genders was encouraged by companies wanting to make a profit by introducing baby style guides. There is an anecdote that, at one point, pink was thought of as a male colour and blue a girl colour. It goes to show that much of the binary associations that we make about genders are arbitrary.

NONBINARY AND TRANSGENDER PEOPLE

The topic of the diversity of gender identities provokes strong debates, which are sprinkled with stories of fear. Some think that embracing nonbinary and transgender identities will somehow force our young people to change gender. This is reminiscent of the homophobic narrative that talking about being gay would encourage our youth to become gay, or even be turned gay (Margaret Thatcher's section 28 still echoes today). Embracing nonbinary gender identities also rocks the boat of the patriarchy, which is invested in "the male" being the dominant one in the family structure. Some may even feel that their entire nuclear family is under attack. Indeed, discussing nonbinary gender identities threatens the existential idea of "man" itself. The term "man" has often been used as a synonym for "human". Perhaps, the acknowledgement of nonbinary gender identities can help us all remind ourselves that all people are humans. Isn't it more important to be human than to be defined by genitals? In fact, it seems that in the vendetta to attack nonbinary and transgender people, and the attempt to take away their rights, we can actually become inhuman.

Most of the negative stories about nonbinary and transgender people happen online or in sensationalised newspapers. In real life, when you actually meet nonbinary and transgender people, you will notice that a great majority of them are peaceful people who only want their existence not to be constantly debated, denied, or dismissed.

A majority of people who have completed gender affirming transition experience no regret and report their mental health improved quickly (Tordoff et al., 2022). Being gender-affirmative is merely listening to what a person is experiencing in the here and now and not telling them that what they're experiencing is wrong. People may have different feelings and thoughts about their gender at different times. Being gender-affirmative is listening to all of it and, in a therapeutic setting, helping a person make sense of themselves.

Gender dysphoria, the dissonance between gender identity and the sex assigned at birth, is distressing for people, but it is not considered a mental health disorder. Some people who feel their gender is different from their biological sex report feeling "tormented" every day and that the only solution to end their torment is gender affirming procedures.

Robert Sapolsky (2017), a professor of biology and neurology writes:

> The dimorphic brain regions in transgender individuals resembled the sex of the person they had always felt themselves to be, not their "actual" sex. In other words, it's not the case that transgender individuals think they're a different gender than they actually are. It's more like they got stuck with the bodies of a different sex from who they actually are.
>
> (2017, p. 215 *footnote*)

Our relationship with our bodies, combined with navigating other challenges in life, can have a significant impact on our sex life and relationships.

Imani (they/them) is a person assigned female at birth and identifying as Black trans-masculine. Their family rejected them when they started to look more "male", which was a major relational trauma for them. They feel tormented by their body every day because it doesn't match who they feel they are. Summer is particularly difficult because the heat demands to wear less clothes and there are less opportunities to hide distressing parts of their body. Their relational trauma from their family's rejection is compounded by the consistent trauma of racism and transphobia. The constant challenge to just exist in the world and get on with life takes an enormous amount of energy, and therefore they feel they have very little energy left to handle the anxiety of dating or having sexual contact with someone.

Currently, the level of transphobia is worrying and on the increase. The UK government's Home Office Official Statistics (2021) show that hate crime against transgender people rose by 3% in the year 2020/2021.

People can become upset when they are required to see beyond their comfort zone of binary gender categories. Terms such as "assigned/assumed female at birth" (AFAB) or "assigned/assumed male at birth" (AMAB) to describe biological sex can be used alongside the genders people identify with: woman, man, nonbinary, and so on. As we become more aware of the large diversities of human beings, it is important to change our language to reflect our expanded awareness. We don't need to live in a world of "either/or" when we can be with "and/and". Although there is a definition for sex and gender that help us differentiate between the two terms, it is worth noting that they are not completely separate things because sex and gender are complex aspects of a person and they interact with each other constantly influencing our ongoing human development. It is much the same as nature and nurture being different things but cannot be separated as both are in a complex relationship to inform a person's ongoing sense of self.

It is OK to admit that we still have much to learn about the diversity of human experiences. All we need to do is keep listening, keep reflecting, and keep learning. Let's show more humility embracing what we don't know rather than staying stuck with our binary certainties.

THE DIFFERENT GENDERS

Let's take a look at the different genders. This is not an exhaustive list and it is important to note that these terms may change over time. Some of these words do not have an official definition that you can find in dictionaries, but there are terms used by the people who self-identify as such. I believe clinical sexologists have a duty to be gender affirming, which means that they need to commit to keeping updated with the current terms. This list is only an introduction to begin to understand the vast spectrum of genders.

Agender is not identifying with a gender. People who are agender may also describe themselves as being "gender-neutral" or "genderless".

Bigender is identifying as two genders. For example male and female, or male and agender, or any other gender combination. There is a wide spectrum of expressions and behaviours depending on individual people.

Cisgender is a person whose gender identity matches the sex assigned at birth. For example, people who are assigned male at birth will express their gender as the traditional expression of being a man and self-identify as a man.

Gender fluid is understood as moving fluidly between genders with their identity shifting between male and female or neither.

People identifying as gender fluid often describe feeling male some days and female on other days, both male and female or neither. Some gender fluid people may also identify as "genderqueer". Others prefer to identify as gender fluid.

Genderqueer is a term that describes being gender non-confirming (or gender fluid). People identifying as genderqueer often reject binary labels. Some prefer to call themselves nonbinary.

Third gender describes a person who does not identify with either man or woman but identifies with another gender, called third gender. The notion of third gender is well established in some cultures but not so much in Western countries. Third gender is not rigidly defined as it can mean different things to different people who identify as such.

Transgender is used as a term to describe a person who identifies their gender as different from the sex they were assigned at birth. Some people prefer to be called trans rather than transgender. Some trans people have medical interventions to change their appearance to better match their gender, such as gender affirming hormone treatments or surgery. Other people do not want surgery, while others are happy to live without medical interventions but with the life that is typically associated with the gender that they identify with.

A note on intersex people: it is a misconception to identify people with intersex characteristics as part of gender diversity as they are actually a part of human biological diversity. In other words, having intersex characteristics describe an embodiment experience rather than a gender expression.

DIFFERENT PRONOUNS

As we recognise that sex and gender are not binary and there is an infinite spectrum between the male and female expressions, we need to update our language in how we address people. It is quite simple: we only need to listen to how people want to be addressed and follow their request. My pronouns are he/him/his. I identify as a cisgender gay man. My name is Silva (but my close friends know they can call me "Darling").

The two typical personal pronouns are:

Identifying as a man: he, him, his, himself
Identifying as a woman: she, her, hers, herself

Some people may wish to be addressed by other pronouns as it matches their gender more accurately than the two typical ones. There are a large number of pronouns that can be used, but the two common ones are:

they, them, theirs, themselves
Ze (or Zie) – (can also be spelt Xe)

Titles of nonbinary people can be altered from the binary Mr/Ms/Mrs to its gender-neutral version Mx, (pronounced "miks").

Taking people's pronouns seriously is important because it makes the difference between accepting or dismissing someone's existence. Have you ever noticed how we are usually very careful not to misgender a baby for fear of offending their parents (especially if the mistake is misgendering a baby boy for a girl)? When someone is pregnant, everybody is anxious to know the sex of the baby. Yet, many people in our society seem not to want to make an effort to use the "they" pronouns with someone who requests it. Isn't it a little strange?

SEXISM

Talking about sex and gender as inclusive terms is good for everybody because it can help with challenging our society's intrinsic sexism.

Sexism is broadly understood as prejudice or discrimination based on gender. It includes stereotyping behaviours or attitudes that are based on binary social roles. Sexism is mostly associated with discrimination against people who identify as women because they are more typically affected by negative impacts based on their gender: equal rights, equal pay, abortion rights, as well as not being taken as seriously in some professions, especially those of leadership, which create what is commonly known as the "glass ceiling". Women, including trans women, have had to fight for their human rights over decades, and the fight still goes on because they are still treated appallingly.

Here are some typical examples of sexism against women:

1. *Not being a mother:* Sophie is 30 years old. She is in a long-term relationship with a loving man. She has decided not to have children. Her friends and family think there is something wrong with her, perhaps she can't have children, but they are not questioning her boyfriend's fertility. Also, they do not accept that choosing not to have children is an affirmative choice that does not mean that "something is wrong" with her. Some friends and family members also called her "selfish" for choosing not to have a child.

2. *Being a mother:* Afia is also 30 years old. She runs her own company and she is becoming quite successful. She doesn't have any time to date and find a suitable partner, but she does want to have a child. She has decided to have a child by herself. Her friends and family criticise her for choosing to be a single parent, as, "surely it is better to have a man by her side?"

3. *Being a mother and working:* Faiza is married to Amir. They are both settled and in their mid-30s. When Faiza gave birth to her baby, she chose to take maternity leave only for two months as she was keen to return to work. Her friends and family could not understand that choice: doesn't she like her baby? Why doesn't she want to nurse her child? They called her "cold", "heartless", "selfish".

4. *Being sexual:* Veronica loves her vibrant sex life. She has sex with multiple partners, watches porn, masturbates on a regular basis, and occasionally enjoys a full weekend visiting sex clubs. She enjoys living on her own and she doesn't want a boyfriend or husband. When she talks about her sex life with others, they tend to call her a "slut", "whore", or "sex addict". They believe something is wrong with her for not wanting to "settle down".

5. *Being successful:* Sakura is a very successful lawyer. She had to fight very hard to get to that position because her firm is male-dominated and she hadn't been taken seriously for many years. In meetings, men would repeat her statements as though it held more weight if they said it, they would sometimes appropriate her original ideas as theirs, and there was a lot of "mansplaining"

going on, too. After working harder than most of the men in the firm, she was finally taken seriously, professionally. But then, the criticism started to change from being looked down on, to being aggressive and intimidating, words that would never be used for her male counterparts when they needed to be assertive. When Sakura goes on a date with men, she is often told that she makes them uncomfortable because she earns more money than them.

6. *Being "boyish"*: Sonia identifies as a heterosexual cisgender woman. She likes her hair short, she doesn't like makeup, and she prefers to wear male clothes. She doesn't particularly enjoy cooking or doing house chores, but she loves car racing, sword fighting, karate, and weightlifting. She's often told that she's "a lesbian in the closet" or she's "scary". She finds it difficult to have a relationship, or even friendships, because people judge her on the way she looks.

7. *Not being a woman*: Rita is a trans woman who identifies as a woman. She has always felt like a woman, from as far back as she can remember. She worries that she doesn't "pass" as a woman because she's taller than the average woman. Many people refuse to accept her identity as a woman (you're not a "real" woman). On a daily basis, she experiences people's judgements because she's trans, as well as the sexism that all women face. However, unlike cisgender women, she doesn't feel welcome in "ladies toilets", which can be a refuge from sexism (and misogyny), because she's perceived as a threat. Rita feels that her very existence is unwelcome and there aren't any safe spaces for her.

Sexism against women is intrinsic in our society. It doesn't matter what women choose to do or not do, they cannot win, because there is always a ghastly label that is put on them. They are sluts if they have a lot of sex. They are frigid if they don't have enough sex. They are spinsters if they decide not to be in a relationship. They are selfish if they don't want to be a mother. They are even more selfish if they choose to be a mother and work at the same time. They are aggressive if they are assertive. They are nagging if they complain. They are intimidating if they earn a lot of money. They are second class if they don't earn enough money. They are not "real" if they are trans women. The list goes on. Sexism is dangerous for women because this discrimination is the fuel to violence against them. The World

Health Organization (WHO): Violence against women (2021) estimates that one in three women worldwide is subjected to physical and/or sexual violence in their lifetime.

However, in its definition, sexism is also a term that describes prejudice towards men (Calder-Dawe and Gavey, 2016). They, too, report suffering from sexism, although there are less of those reports, perhaps because the sexist stereotype of men needing to be strong stops them from speaking up about their suffering.

Here are some examples of sexism against them:

1. *Being emotional*: Bruno is an artist and an empath. He often feels sad, which he calls melancholia, not depression. He has made friends with his melancholia by expressing it through his art. He describes being unsuccessful on dates with women because he doesn't earn enough money. His friends and family are exasperated with him, telling him he should "toughen up" or "man-up" because he's "too sensitive".

2. *Being masculine*: Azibo identifies as a heterosexual cisgender man. He has a good job and manages his life well. He also enjoys going to beauty salons on a regular basis to have facials, manicures, and pedicures. His friends and family think he's weird for enjoying that, and they worry that perhaps he's "gay and in the closet". He also enjoys putting on some eyeliner when he goes to a party. He sometimes fears being attacked for it. He finds it difficult to meet a girlfriend who is willing to accept those things that are not typically masculine.

3. *Being feminine*: Hiroshi also identifies as a heterosexual cisgender man, and he identifies as a cross-dresser. He feels his very best when he wears tights, a skirt, and stilettos. He usually does this at home, by himself, at the weekend because he's not comfortable coming out about this. He has not managed to find a romantic partner who is willing to accept his crossdressing as they usually think he's gay or "bizarre".

4. *Being the breadwinner*: Scott works in a highly stressful and demanding company. He has a major decision-making role and often has to work long hours to manage time-zone differences when having meetings with people in other countries, and he sometimes has to work weekends too. He earns a very good salary but he doesn't like his work at all. He feels the pressure

to keep earning for doing something that he feels is soul-destroying because he is supposed to be the man of the family. His wife, who doesn't work, expects Scott to continue to earn the same salary to maintain their luxurious lifestyle and the financial commitment to have their two children in private school. He gets much praise for being the man of the family from his wife, his friends, and his family but there is no room to discuss the emotional and psychological cost to him. He is expected to "get on with it".

5. *Being a good lover*: Esteban struggles with his erections because he feels anxious when he is in a sexual situation with a woman. He has grown up to believe that men should always be good lovers and they should always have erections on demand. He believes that it is natural and easy to have erections when a woman undresses in front of him and he feels "broken" for not managing it. When he meets his friends in the pub, they all talk about their sexual prowess and the amazing orgasms they give their sexual partners. He also hears from his friends that the more women you conquer, the more desirable you are. Esteban doesn't feel this way at all. He'd prefer to take things slowly, get to know a woman, and be monogamous. He also doesn't want all the sexual activities to focus on his hard penis. He feels he is "strange" and "less of a man" because of that.

6. *Being tall*: Patrick is 5'4" tall. He is shorter than all his friends and family members. He has struggled to be taken seriously all his life because of his height. Many people make jokes about it and he is expected to laugh and take it on the chin, but expressing his feelings of hurt and sadness is not welcome. He finds it difficult to date and meet people who want to be with him because of his height. In order to be accepted, he feels he needs to be the joker or the clown as it is the only way for him to be seen and liked.

7. *Being a man*: Diego is a cisgender gay man and a wheelchair user. When he goes out with his non-disabled husband, people speak to his husband to address him. For example, in a restaurant, the staff would ask his husband what Diego wants to order. If they speak to Diego directly, they would use a tone of voice as

though they spoke to an infant, not a man. People also assume that his husband is his professional paid carer, they are shocked when they're told he is his partner.

Men do suffer from sexism too because there are many strict and damaging messages of what masculinity should look like. One of the most pervasive messages is not to be weak, which means not to show vulnerability. This is harmful to many men because they are less likely to open up to someone or to go to therapy. When their unprocessed emotions become unbearable, they are more likely to resort to self-harm, and, tragically, suicide. According to the Office for National Statistics (2021), men ending their own lives represent three-quarters of all suicide deaths in England and Wales (www.ons.gov.uk).

Men can also be victims to global stereotyping statements such as "all men are cheaters", "men only think with their dicks", "the best way to get to a man's heart is through his stomach", and so on, portraying men as emotionally immature who only respond to basic animal instincts. This isn't helpful.

The gender-bias roles that we are conditioned to believe are powerful and still very much part of the fabric of our society. If sexism remains unchallenged, it can subconsciously inform our behaviours and attitudes, and we can put pressure on ourselves and others to conform to some gender roles that might not fit who we are, thus creating problems. If we can all learn to think in less binary ways about women and men, femininity and masculinity, we may reduce the harm done to all genders and our world may become a better, gentler and safer place to be for everybody.

MISOGYNY

Misogyny describes a blanket dislike (or hate) towards women. Misogyny also affects trans women, called trans-misogyny. The everyday sexism against women fuels contempt towards them and can transform into misogyny. Just like sexism against women, misogyny is intrinsic in our society, so much so that it has disturbingly become part of our normal. The most visible symptom of misogyny is the high prevalence of rape and violence against women. The Crime

Survey for England and Wales (CSEW) – Office for National Statistics (2021) reported that 84 per cent of all sexual offences recorded by the police in the year ending March 2020 were against women.

Unfortunately, misogyny extends even further into society's everyday contempt for women. Here are some examples:

1. *Women as objects*: it is so common to hear women speak about being touched inappropriately. A number of women report being touched on their shoulders, knees, or even their breasts and buttocks without consent. Women are also raised to not make a fuss so, most of the time, they don't complain about it, but it doesn't mean they are not uncomfortable about it. Also, men do not tend to be touched in that way so society's message is that the physical integrity of the bodies of women is not worthy of respect compared with the bodies of men. It's also sending the message that women can be used as objects for the gaze of men and their sexual pleasure. The same problems extend to trans women who frequently report people with inappropriate behaviours towards their bodies. Many blame pornography for this. Although much of mainstream heterosexual pornography is distasteful for women, misogyny predates online porn by centuries. Let's address the real issue: the way we raise our children that colludes with misogyny and makes it "normal".

2. *Women and sexual pleasure*: Women's sexual pleasure has largely been dismissed for decades. It is only now, in the 21st century, that we are starting to pay attention to women's sexual pleasure, and there is still a long way to go. It seems ironic given that the clitoris is the only organ in the human body that exists for the sole purpose of pleasure, as you will see in Chapter 5. Traditionally, women are raised to "please their man" and men are raised to "conquer" women. These messages play an enormous part in how people choose to be in a relationship with each other. So many women report tolerating sex, without feeling empowered to say "stop" if the sexual activity doesn't feel good. Men tend to think that their ejaculation means the end of sex, no matter if their sexual partner has reached orgasm or not. Men expect women to spend a considerable amount of time with oral sex on their penis, but there is little reciprocation.

3. *Women, age, and beauty*: women are only worthy when they are young, and they can be dismissed (or binned) as soon as they

age. This is part of the same narrative as women being objects for the gaze of men. It's also part of women needing to be beautiful. If women do not conform to the beauty standard that society approves of, they are invisible or dismissed, no matter how old they are. Larger women can be funny but not sexy (although this is beginning to change, thankfully). Many women are vulnerable to spending an enormous amount of money on diets and cosmetic surgery for that reason. However, even the women who reach the beauty standard are not safe for long. As soon as they age a little (meaning past 40 years of age), they are also tossed aside and disregarded. Again, this is changing slowly thanks to brilliant stars like Helen Mirren who is unapologetically sexy in her mid-70s.

4. *Women and safety*: Our culture of contempt towards women also informs the attitudes society holds regarding the responsibility for their safety. Too often, we have heard of women being blamed for being raped: they shouldn't have got drunk, they wore too short a dress, they led the man on, they acted "slutty", they shouldn't have let them inside their house, and so on. When there is media coverage of a woman being murdered, we suddenly hear what women should change in order to be safer: don't walk alone at night, hold your keys in your hand as a weapon, call someone, learn karate … but how often do we discuss what men can do to change? For example, men can learn to challenge the unhelpful messages of masculinity between them, respect women's rights and their bodily integrity, speak to them as equal human beings.

How much does sexism against women fuel everyday misogyny? Let's take a closer look:

1. *Fairy tales*: the young woman from a poor background has to wait to be picked by the prince so that she can become a princess. Or the young princess is helpless and needs to be rescued by the warrior (who is a man).

2. *Films*: the woman is chased by a murderer, but they are so stupid that they run upstairs to the attic where there is no exit rather than out of the front door. If, by chance, they had a weapon in their hand, they will throw it away. If a young woman is sexual at the beginning of a film, you can be sure she will be the first victim, usually of a gruesome death. I'm sure we can all

remember some films in which trans women are portrayed as dangerous psychopaths.

3. *Life*: notice what questions women get asked that men don't. For example, "Why don't you have children?", "Why aren't you married?", "Why can't you keep a man?", "What diet have you been on lately?" and, "Can you handle your alcohol?"

Misogyny is closely linked with what we call "toxic masculinity". Some men don't like that term because they think it means "all men are bad", but this is not correct. Toxic masculinity is not a criticism of men as human beings, but it is a collection of ideas, attitudes, and behaviours that some men adopt. The messages of toxic masculinity inform those men that having any weakness is wrong because it is associated with women, so anything that feminises men is to be rejected. Some disabled men can be particularly wounded by the messages of toxic masculinity as their masculinity is erased for being "inferior", further adding to the difficulty in feeling "good enough" to find a partner or having a satisfying sex life.

Some of the traits of "toxic masculinity" are:

1. Enduring physical and emotional pain in silence.
2. Having no need for warmth, comfort, love, or tenderness.
3. Having no emotions other than bravery and anger. Any emotions might be perceived as weakness. Weakness is absolutely unacceptable.
4. Not depending on anyone. Asking for help is also perceived as a weakness. Feeling connected and needing someone else's open arms is also unacceptable.
5. Always winning, no matter what, whether it is sport, work, relationships, or sex.

As you can imagine, toxic masculinity hurts women and it hurts the very men who adopt it too.

MISANDRY

Misandry describes a blanket dislike (or hate) towards men. Although it is less visible and definitely not as intrinsic in our society as misogyny, because of the high value society places on patriarchy, it does not mean it is not a problem to seriously consider. There are some people on Twitter who call for action such as "kill all men". Part of the narrative of men that is "they should get on with things and not be vulnerable" means that some violence and hatred towards men may go unnoticed and not taken so seriously. For example, cases of domestic violence perpetrated by a man towards a woman are considered very serious, but the reverse is not perceived as such. Indeed, women can do serious bodily harm to men. The Crime Survey for England and Wales (year ending March 2020) estimates 3.6 per cent (757,000) of men were victims of domestic abuse. Many men don't report being abused by women because they feel ashamed to admit it, and fear being mocked by their peers.

There are fewer reports and, therefore, fewer examples of misandry compared to misogyny, so it is not so obvious. Although misandry very much exists, it happens in some small, select groups and is not intrinsically part of our society, our fairy tales, our stories, and the everyday lives of most people. Here are some situations in which misandry can play a part:

1. Tabloids regale in "juicy" stories of celebrities cheating on their wives, calling them "perverts", "pigs", or "sex addicts".
2. Much of the media have sensationalist stories on shaming men who watch pornography, at best making them the object of mockery (the "wanker"), and at worst, accusing them of being bad people, with some dark and twisted sex brain, who will most probably sexually offend.
3. Some peer-led programmes, for women who have been betrayed by men, can be dangerous misandry breeding spaces where women will spend their time encouraging each other's anger and rage towards men.

SUMMARY

It is important to be aware that most of what we were told about men and women, masculinity and femininity, are stories based on the re-writing of history through the Western lens rather than seeing the bigger picture of the diverse world, where some cultures have not adopted such binary ways of structuring their societies. So much of what we think we know about sex and gender seems problematic, leaving us with beliefs of binary thinking that can fuel sexism, misogyny, and misandry, and therefore harm everybody. By contrast, embracing that humans are not binary is good for everybody. It helps challenge some of the things we believe to be true and rock the boat of patriarchy. It can help people have a better sex life, better relationships and friendships, and it can also save lives. All we need to do is be humble, and keep opening our minds, and hearts, to the amazing diversity of human beings.

Reflective questions:

1 What informs your thoughts and feelings about femininity and masculinity?

2 What informs your self-identification and what words do you choose to describe yourself?

3 What are the situations or circumstances when you feel you have to edit parts of yourself in order to conform or be accepted?

4 What are the messages you have learnt in childhood about boys and girls?

5 How does your social class, financial position, profession, skin colour, accent, values, nationality, and faith inform your sense of self? Are you aware of how you interact with your intersectionality depending on the here-and-now situation?

6 What are you prejudiced about?

7 What are your automatic thoughts and feelings when you see someone whose looks, behaviours, or attitudes puzzle you?

8 What happens for you when you notice that you have a judgemental thought?

9 How do you understand your gender? How does it inform your behaviours, attitudes, relationships, and sex life?

FURTHER READING

How to Understand Your Gender. A practical guide for exploring who you are, by Alex Iantaffi and Meg-John Barker (2018).

Life Isn't Binary. On Being Both, Beyond, And In-Between, by Meg-John Barker and Alex Iantaffi (2019).

Gender Trauma. Healing Cultural, Social, and Historical Gendered Trauma, by Alex Iantaffi (2021).

REFERENCES

Calder-Dawe, O., & Gavey, N. (2016). Making Sense of Everyday Sexism: Young People and the Gendered Contours of Sexism. *Women's Studies International Forum*, 55, 1–9, ISSN 0277-5395, doi: 10.1016/j.wsif.2015.11.004

dsdfamilies (2019). Stories of Sex Development. [Available Online]: https://dsdfamilies.org

Home Office Official Statistics: Hate Crime, England and Wales 2020 to 2021 (2021). [Available Online]: https://www.gov.uk/government/statistics/hate-crime-england-and-wales-2020-to-2021/hate-crime-england-and-wales-2020-to-2021

Iantaffi, A. (2021). *Gender Trauma. Healing Cultural, Social and Historical Gendered Trauma*. Jessica Kingsley Publishers. London.

Jones, T., Hart, B., Carpenter, M., Ansara, G., Leonard, W., & Lucke, J. (2016). *Intersex: Stories and Statistics from Australia*. Open Book Publishers. Cambridge.

Office for National Statistics (2021). Suicides in England and Wales: 2020 registrations. [Available Online]: https://www.ons.gov.uk/peoplepopulationandcommunity/birthsdeathsandmarriages/deaths/bulletins/suicidesintheunitedkingdom/2020registrations#suicides-in-england-and-wales

Office for National Statistics (2019). What is the difference between sex and gender. [Available Online]: https://www.ons.gov.uk/economy/environmentalaccounts/articles/whatisthedifferencebetweensexandgender/2019-02-21

Office for National Statistics (n.d.). Domestic abuse. [Available Online]: https://www.ons.gov.uk/peoplepopulationandcommunity/crimeandjustice/articles/domesticabusevictimcharacteristicsenglandandwales/yearendingmarch2020

Sapolsky, R. (2017). *Behave. The Biology of Humans at Our Best and Worst*. Vintage. London.

Sexual assault crime by The Crime Survey for England and Wales (CSEW) (2021) – Office for National Statistics (2021). [Available Online]: https://www.ons.gov.uk/peoplepopulationandcommunity/crimeandjustice/articles/sexualoffencesvictimcharacteristicsenglandandwales/march2020

Soh, D. (2020). *The End of Gender. Debunking the myths about sex and identity in our society*. Threshold Editions. New York.

Tordoff, D.M., Wanta, J.W., Collin, A., Stepney, C., Inwards-Breland, D.J., Ahrens, K. (2022). Mental Health Outcomes in Transgender and Nonbinary Youths Receiving Gender-Affirming Care. *JAMA Netw Open*. 5(2), e220978. doi:10.1001/jamanetworkopen.2022.0978

World Health Organization (WHO): Violence against women (2021). [Available Online]: https://www.who.int/news-room/fact-sheets/detail/violence-against-women

SEXUALITY

In this chapter, I will explore sexuality diversity by looking at some of the most common sexual orientations. In the next chapter, you will read about eroticism, as part of our Erotic Template and specific turn-ons. While sexual orientations and eroticism can be intertwined, they are different.

SEXUAL ORIENTATION AND EROTICISM

Sexual orientation is innate, not learnt. It describes a consistent emotional, romantic and/or sexual attraction. Some sexual orientations include sexual, emotional and/or romantic attraction to people of the same gender (gay), people of a different gender from their own (heterosexual), people that are similar to and different from their own gender (bisexual), all genders (pansexual) or neither (asexual). For the majority of people, sexual orientation is fixed for life, but for others, it can change over time. Moser (2016) defines the different characteristics of sexual orientations: (1) Lust: a strong and persistent sexual attraction; (2) Relative immutability: emerges in childhood or early puberty and is relatively constant throughout life; (3) Flexibility: despite being relatively constant, sexual interests might change over time. We don't have control over whether our sexuality changes or not; (4) Consequences: the outcome of embracing our sexual orientation has profound psychological well-being.

Sexual orientation is separate from gender. Nichols (2021) writes:

Sexual orientation doesn't change when people transition, but the label will change. In other words, someone assigned male at

DOI: 10.4324/9781003276913-4

birth and attracted to women will be perceived as heterosexual before they transition, but once they are trans women – they are lesbians!

(2021, p. 183)

Eroticism, on the other hand, is both innate and created; it is more changeable over the course of one's life. With eroticism, it is possible to explore the question "why am I turned on by this or that?" Although there isn't always a reason for some of our turn-ons, it is also possible to make sense of some of them. By contrast, sexual orientations just are – and there is no "why?" Through affirmative exploration, it is possible to make some sense and meaning of how we experience our sexual and romantic attractions in accepting that it is part of the diversity of human beings.

SEXUAL ORIENTATION DIVERSITIES

Here are some of the words that are currently used to describe diverse sexual orientations:

Asexuality: generally means having no sexual attraction. It is a broad spectrum, which includes varying degrees of attractions, from none at all to sometimes, and, with some people, only to a certain type of people or in specific circumstances. Asexuality, as well as all sexual orientations, describes the attraction, not necessarily the desire. Some asexual people may feel sexual desire but not enough attraction to motivate them to have sex. An absence of sexual attraction does not mean an absence of romantic attraction. Many asexual people want to be in an intimate and romantic relationship (or several relationships) with other people, but not have sex with them. Being asexual is different from being abstinent. Abstinence is a choice, usually underpinned by values (mostly religious ones). Abstinent people often experience sexual attraction to others but choose not to act on them. Asexual people don't have the sexual attraction in the first place and the thought of having sex simply doesn't make sense to some of them. Some asexual people also identify as heterosexual, gay, queer, bisexual, pansexual, and an intersection of other sexual orientations. Within the umbrella of asexuality, there are other terms that some people prefer to self-identify with, such as:

Cupiosexual: people who don't experience sexual and/or romantic attraction but still desire to engage in sexual behaviours or have a sexual relationship.

Graysexual: people who experience sexual attraction either infrequently or not very intensely.

Grayromantic: people who experience romantic attraction rarely or not very strongly.

Demisexual: people who feel sexual attraction towards people with whom they have already established a strong emotional bond. Some people who are demisexual may have no interest or a slight interest in sexual activities while others may be polyamorous, and interested in sex as long as there is a strong emotional bond first. Demisexual people tend to regard friendship very highly and their sexual attraction often springs up from friendship.

Autosexuality: people who experience a sexual attraction towards themselves. This is often misunderstood because people often think that autosexual people are narcissists or arrogant, and are only interested in themselves when having sex. This is not the case with autosexual people because they also experience sexual attraction towards other people, and therefore can simultaneously enjoy their bodies and others'. For example, Tony loves his body and he loves connecting physically with his girlfriend's body. His best sexual experiences are when he can have sex with his girlfriend in front of a large mirror. He gets so turned on by both his body and his girlfriend's that he becomes his best sexual self, engaging meaningfully with his girlfriend. On the other hand, a narcissist or an arrogant person would be looking at their body in the mirror and not paying that much attention to their sexual partner (it can be a very boring sexual experience for the partner). Autosexual people tend to like looking after their bodies, feeling proud of them. They may also like to take videos of their sexual activities either with solo sex or partnered sex. Autosexual people can also self-identify with other sexual orientations: heterosexual, gay, bisexual, pansexual, and so on.

Bicurious: describes people who identify as heterosexual and who are interested in having a sexual or romantic experience with someone of the same gender. For some people, the curiosity stays in their fantasies. For example, John identifies as bicurious because part of his identity is a heterosexual cisgender man in a happy relationship with his wife and he enjoys masturbating to porn featuring gay men. For some people, they enjoy the *idea* of being touched sexually by someone of the same gender but do not follow through to actual touch in real life.

Bisexuality: describes people who are emotionally, sexually and/or romantically attracted to people of the same gender and different gender from their own. Some bisexual people would strongly identify with the meaning of "bi" as in "two" and the word "sex" as in biological sex and would see themselves as sexually, emotionally, and/or romantically attracted to two binary sexes of people assigned male/female at birth. Others would accept a definition of being attracted to more than one gender, moving them closer to a pansexual or polysexual identity (see below). A person can be bisexual and have a monogamous relationship code.

Digisexuality: is an emerging sexual orientation that sex researchers are starting to explore (McArthur & Twist, 2017). This term describes people who are emotionally, sexually, and/or romantically attracted to other people through devices and technology. Some people feel the most fulfilled when they can connect with other human beings through a device or a screen. This allows for international relationships as well as sexual behaviours free of sexually transmitted infections. There are two types of people identifying with digisexuality: people who enjoy interacting with other human beings through a device (preferring masturbating to porn rather than having partnered sex, or those who enjoy cyber/cam sex); and people who enjoy sex with devices that don't involve other human beings (alternative reality), and eventually, when it becomes more financially accessible, sex and intimate relationships with robots.

Gay: is a term encompassing people who are emotionally, sexually and/or romantically attracted towards people of the same gender. There is a large diversity of gay people, including many who also identify with specific erotic turn-ons (see Chapter 4). The term "gay" is often used as an umbrella term that includes gay men and women. Some people prefer to identify as MSM (men who have sex with men), and WSW (women who have sex with women). There are some people who identify as heterosexual who sometimes have sex with people of the same gender. The term "gay" is a word that describes a community too, identified by the rainbow flag, also called the "progress flag" (which includes all LGBTQ+ people).

Heterosexuality: also called "straight", are people who are emotionally, sexually, and/or romantically attracted to their binary opposite sex or a different gender from their own. Heterosexuality doesn't always mean "straight" as there is a wide range of sexual diversity in heterosexual people. Some heterosexual people can be on the spectrum of asexuality. Some heterosexual people have specific kink and fetish and may also identify as "queer" because they don't fit with the typical heterosexuality that society prescribes (see Chapter 4). Some heterosexual people love to lead the "typical heterosexual life" (getting married to someone of the binary opposite gender and having children) while others don't want that life at all. Some embrace the term "straight", while others dislike it.

Lesbian: refers to a woman who has emotional, sexual, and/or romantic attraction towards women. Some people prefer the term "gay woman" while others prefer "lesbian".

Monosexuality: is an umbrella term encompassing all sexual orientations that feel an emotional, sexual, and/or romantic attraction towards only one gender. People who identify as monosexual usually identify as exclusively heterosexual, gay, or lesbian.

Multisexuality: is the opposite of monosexuality. It describes people of all sexual orientations who are emotionally, sexually, and/or romantically attracted to more than one gender.

Omnisexuality: refers to people who are emotionally, sexually, and/or romantically attracted to people of all genders. Unlike pansexuality (see below), omnisexual people recognise the gender of potential partners (which means that genders matter to them).

Pansexuality: those who identify as pansexual feel attraction to people without noticing their gender. In other words, it could be said that pansexual people are "gender blind", unlike omnisexual people.

Polysexuality: people who identify their sexual orientation as polysexual also are emotionally, sexually, and/or romantically attracted to all genders. Gender may or may not be a factor for their attraction. Although they may be attracted to people of multiple genders, they're not attracted to people of all genders.

Pomosexuality: describes people who reject all labels that attempt to define sexuality and gender. Pomosexual people emphasise that the term itself should not constitute a definition of a sexuality. I'm aware that by including pomosexuality on this list of "sexual orientations" is contradictory to their philosophy. I apologise.

Queer: is a word used for people from the LGBTQ+ communities who identify as such. The term "queer" used to be an insult towards the LGBTQ+ people. It has since been reclaimed from within the LGBTQ+ community as a way to celebrate sexual diversities and not conform to heteronormativity. The term "queer" can still be an offensive word if used as a deliberate insult against a person who is part of the LGBTQ+ community. People who identify as being queer often connect to more than a sexual attraction, it also has a cultural meaning.

Sapiosexuality: describes people who are primarily emotionally, sexually, and/or romantically attracted to intelligence. Some sapiosexual people can identify as heterosexual, gay, bisexual, or any of the other sexual orientation descriptors.

DIVERSITIES WITHIN SEXUAL ORIENTATIONS

It is important to understand that everybody is on a sexual orientation spectrum (as explained by the Kinsey Scale), which means that people will experience their sexuality differently from another who identifies with the same sexual orientation. There is infinite diversity in the experiencing of sexuality. Barker and Iantaffi (2019) gift us with the most brilliant explanation of sexuality diversity:

> We might make an analogy with our taste of hot beverages. We could create a Kinsey-style scale from our tea to coffee, with people who prefer tea at one end, coffee at the other, and people who like both in the middle. But, of course, liking tea more doesn't necessarily make us like coffee less. Where do we put people who really *love* their morning coffee and their afternoon

tea? What about people who are pretty "meh" on both drinks. In fact what about people who'd prefer a cup of hot chocolate?

(2019, p. 31)

Within the sexual orientations above, some people's attractions to specific genders may include the physical aspects of them (penis, vulva, breasts, body hair, etc.) but some people are attracted to gender expressions, as in masculinity, femininity, and nonbinary, rather than the physical parts.

Androphilia: People who are emotionally, sexually and/or romantically attracted to masculinity. For example, a heterosexual man who finds women who are "manly" attractive. Or gay men who are turned on by masculine men, or gay men who are attracted by masculine trans men who may have a vulva.

Gynephilia: People who are emotionally, sexually, and/or romantically attracted to femininity. For example, a heterosexual man who loves women who are feminine. Gay men who are attracted to feminine men (these men are not necessarily anally receptive, but they may have behaviours that are typically feminine, like enjoying wearing some make-up). Or a lesbian who is attracted to feminine women.

Skoliosexual: People who are emotionally, sexually, and/or romantically attracted to people who are nonbinary, transgender, or gender-queer. For example, someone who is attracted to people who express their masculinity and femininity equally, or people who are agender, or people who identify as trans.

Dr Fritz Klein (1993–2012) developed the *Klein Sexual Orientation Grid (KSOG)*, which is more sophisticated than the Kinsey Scale as it acknowledges more variables in people's experience of their sexuality, including a scale of past, present, and ideal, acknowledging the continuum of sexual orientations. The variables are: (1) sexual attraction; (2) sexual behaviour; (3) sexual fantasies; (4) emotional preference; (5) social preference; (6) heterosexual/gay lifestyle, (in the context of social interactions); (7) self-identification. Through the KSOG, we can become more aware of the multiple ways that people experience their sexual orientations.

Darragh self-identifies as heterosexual because he identifies as a cisgender man who is emotionally, sexually, and romantically attracted to women. His sexual behaviours match his self-identified sexual orientations. He occasionally fantasises about same-sex touch. He loves being emotionally close to women in a romantic sense, but also experiences a different kind of emotional need by being hugged by men. His social network is entirely heterosexual and his lifestyle is one that is associated with typical heterosexuality.

Chiyo self-identifies as bisexual. Her current sexual behaviours are typically heterosexual because she is in a monogamous relationship with a man. She often fantasises about sex with women and masturbates to those fantasies (as well as memories of her past sexual experiences with women). She is romantically connected with her boyfriend and does not wish to be romantically involved with anyone else at the moment. Her social network comprises people of all gender and sexual orientation identities. She attends Pride events every year.

Adrian self-identifies as a gay man. His emotional, romantic, and sexual behaviours are congruent with his self-identification, he also only fantasises about sex with men. Adrian identifies with being an androphile, finding masculinity very attractive. His social network is made of gay men and heterosexual women as he feels he can connect and relate with them more than other populations.

Sandro also identifies as a cisgender gay man. In his own life, he embraces his sense of masculinity and femininity. He occasionally enjoys wearing make-up or painting his nails. Erotically, Sandro identifies as an androphile, he is highly turned on by masculinity. He loves what he calls "the male body". In his erotic fantasies, the "male body" alone is sufficient to be arousing, which means he doesn't need to consider any other traits, such as personality. However, romantically, he is particularly attracted to men who are highly intellectual and also what he describes as "emotionally intelligent", which means men who are in touch with their emotions and can express them well, thus identifying romantically as sapiosexual. His social network comprises intellectual queer and heterosexual people, and he describes his lifestyle as "gay" because he enjoys having queer artwork in his house.

Rafiki self-identifies as heterosexual. He is sexually and romantically attracted to nonbinary people and trans women. He keeps this a secret as his social network is entirely heterosexual and cisgender, and he believes they won't understand his romantic and sexual attraction. He fantasises about being able to marry a nonbinary person or a trans woman.

SEXUALITY DIVERSITIES AND THE HETERONORMATIVE SOCIETY

The definition of heteronormativity is the assumption that people who are heterosexual are "normal" and those who are not are "abnormal" or "weird" (Barker, 2018). Heteronormativity is not only about heterosexual orientations but about the strict code of what is deemed an acceptable lifestyle, which typically means being a cisgender, heterosexual, and monogamous person whose best achievement is to have children, and who enjoys penis-in-vagina penetration with their committed partner at the frequency of not too much, not too little. Having this life vision is not problematic in itself, in fact, many people love having that life, but what is problematic is imposing that vision as the gold standard for humankind and judging others as "not as good", "alternative" or "wrong" based on those values.

Living in a world in which heteronormativity isn't challenged presents significant issues in the everyday lives of people whose identity is outside of those expectations. Meyer (2003) proposes a definition of a particular type of stress called "minority stress", describing it as chronic stress that LGBTQ+ people face on a regular basis due to living in a heteronormative world. Minority stress includes: (1) experiences of prejudice; (2) expectations of rejection; (3) hiding; (4) concealing; (5) internalised homophobia.

The heteronormative world also affects heterosexual people, because heteronormativity isn't a synonym for heterosexuality. Heterosexual people have the pressure to conform to rigid ways of living in order to feel "good enough". Some heterosexual people fear stepping out of the rules that society prescribes for them. For example, a heterosexual couple who choose not to have children can be considered selfish. A heterosexual couple who decide not to live together are considered strange or eccentric.

Asexual people are invisible in society because nobody cares about single people who are not overtly sexual, or they are pathologised as having "sexual aversion". Some even assume that asexual people are not interested in sex because they have been sexually abused, implying they're broken and they should "fix" themselves. Many asexual people are not taken seriously, as though having a sexual relationship is a synonym to maturity, and if people don't have sex, or never had sex, they are grossly infantilised. It is obvious that our society privileges couples over single people: the table for one at the restaurant is usually the one hidden by the toilet door. Going on holiday as a single person requires a surcharge. Most things are packaged for two.

Bisexual people are also invisible. If they are in a relationship with someone of a different gender, they are perceived by everybody to be heterosexual. If they are in a same-gender relationship, they are perceived to be gay. Yet, the reality is that all along they remain bisexual. Bisexual people are often criticised for being "greedy", people who "can't make up their minds", or people who are "gay and in the closet".

Gay people, on top of the minority stress, have to face the ongoing coming out each time they meet someone new who assumes they are heterosexual. When gay men come out, others may start to address them differently, including asking inappropriate sexual questions they wouldn't ask a heterosexual person (What do you do in bed? Who's the top and bottom? Who's the woman in the relationship? etc.), as well as making inappropriate jokes (Hey, you know all about Kylie Minogue, don't you? Do you want to be my girlfriend's best friend? She needs a shopping buddy, etc.)

Lesbian/gay women have their fair share of prejudice, too, with myths of the "lesbian death bed", which means that lesbians are assumed to stop having sex as soon as they commit to a relationship. Some gay women are categorised by the way they look: "the lipstick lesbian" or the "butch lesbian". Some might even make inappropriate jokes ("Wow, you put on make-up, you really don't look like a lesbian", "Lesbians shouldn't have long nails!"). Some lesbians have to endure being fetishised by heterosexual men as part of their sexual fantasies, thinking that it is OK to ask lesbians to have sex in front of them for their own sexual gratification.

SUMMARY

We are all on a spectrum of sexual orientations, which have infinite combinations. It is not a matter of leaning towards heterosexuality or same-gender attraction, but more about the wide diversity that may exist between all of these orientations. The heteronormative world, a rigid type of thinking and rules regarding what is right and what should be wrong, is one of the major problems that induce shame and unhappiness in people's lives. As we are in the 21st century, and we are becoming more and more aware of the amazing diversity of humankind, all of us can challenge those old-fashioned heteronormative messages because they do hurt everybody.

Reflective questions:

1 What comes up for you when you encounter someone who describes a sexual orientation that you don't know about or have never experienced?

2 Are you fully aware of all the different aspects of your sexual orientation?

3 Have you got some pre-conceived judgements or assumptions about some sexual orientations?

4 What are the rules that you have taken on without questioning them based on how you identify your sexual orientation?

5 If you have thoughts that contain "should", "shouldn't", "must", "mustn't" regarding your behaviours matching your sexual orientation identity, how would you rephrase those thoughts without using those words?

6 Are there some rules of society you believe to be true that make you feel bad, unhappy, dismissed? If so, can you think about those rules differently?

FURTHER READING

Perv, The Sexual Deviant in All of Us by Jesse Bering (2013).

The Tragedy of Heterosexuality by Jane Ward (2020).

How to Understand Your Sexuality. A practical guide for exploring who you are by Meg-John Barker and Alex Iantaffi (2022).

REFERENCES

Barker, M.J. (2018). *The Psychology of Sex*. Routledge. Abingdon, Oxon.

Barker, M.J., & Iantaffi, A. (2019). *Life Isn't Binary. On Being Both, Beyond, and In-Between*. Jessica Kingsley Publishers. London.

Klein, F. (1993–2012). *The Bisexual Option*. Second ed. American Institute of Bisexuality, Inc.

McArthur, N., & Twist, M.L.C. (2017). The Rise of Digisexuality: Therapeutic Challenges and Possibilities. *Sexual and Relationship Therapy*, 32(3/4), 334–344.

Meyer, I.H. (2003). Prejudice, Social Stress, and Mental Health in Lesbian, Gay, and Bisexual Populations: Conceptual Issues and Research Evidence. *Psychological Bulletin*, 129(5), 674–697. doi:10.1037/0033-2909.129.5.674

Moser, C. (2016). Defining Sexual Orientation. *Archives of Sexual Behavior*, 45, 505–508. doi:10.1007/s10508-015-0625-y

Nichols, M. (2021). *The Modern Clinician's Guide to Working with LGBTQ+ Clients. The Inclusive Psychotherapist*. Routledge. New York.

EROTICISM

Having explained the wide diversity of sexual orientations in the previous chapter, let us now explore eroticism.

Eroticism encompasses the rich and colourful landscape of our erotic mind, which I call our "Erotic Template" (Neves, 2021). It is important to get to know our own eroticism because it is an integral part of understanding our sexual desires, arousals, and behaviours. We can define eroticism as our erotic orientations within our sexual orientation. To summarise, our sexual orientation describes *who* we are emotionally, romantically, and sexually attracted to, and our eroticism refers to *how* we are emotionally, romantically, and sexually attracted. Our sexual orientation is the frame, our eroticism is the content.

We commonly describe our eroticism as our "turn-ons". Our Erotic Template looks like a painter's palette (Neves, 2021), where you can find many different colours: some colours are dominant on the palette and there are also some minuscule spots of different colours here and there. Some colours are well-defined, while others are mixed up with other colours. The dominant colours are often set for life and don't change much. Some colours may change over the years because our eroticism is fluid, more so than our sexual orientation. Our eroticism evolves with the sexual and romantic experiences we have. For example, a cisgender man who identifies as heterosexual will most likely remain heterosexual even if he had bad experiences with cisgender women, but if he experimented with a sexual position that didn't turn him on, he would be less likely to repeat that particular activity. If he tried something that did turn him on a lot,

DOI: 10.4324/9781003276913-5

he would be more likely to want to repeat it and that particular turn-on might expand on his erotic palette.

It's almost the same as expanding our food palette. The more we try new foods we like from different cuisines, the wider our palette becomes. At the same time, there is no pressure to try everything or to expand our palette beyond what we think is reasonable. Although some people love fried insects, it is not something I ever want to try and I'm quite happy not to expand my palette in that direction. I'm fond of cheese, and as it is strong in my palette, I can find many creative ways to incorporate it in many dishes, or, indeed, in my food fantasies! We don't have control over the fluidity of our sexual orientation, but we can influence how our eroticism develops. Someone's intense turn-on can be another person's repulsion. There are no turn-ons that are better than others, as long as they are consensual and safe.

THE EROTIC TEMPLATE

The Erotic Template is made of memories of sexual experiences and erotic fantasies, some that might have been tried in sexual behaviours, and some never acted upon. The Erotic Template is made of all the elements of our erotic mind that is sexually arousing and erotically potent. Sexual behaviours within the Erotic Template feel pleasurable, fulfilling, and are well-being enhancing. The content of our Erotic Template is not always obvious, so it is important to explore it and be curious about it, but it is equally important not to criticise it. Often, people who are turned on by something or someone that is unusual may think there is something "wrong" with them, believing they are the only ones feeling that way. The reality is that your turn-ons are probably more common than you think. Jesse Bering, in his funny, yet sexologically robust book, *Perv, The Sexual Deviant in All Of Us* (2013) writes:

> He was far more interested in fellating my toes than he was in doing anything with some other body part of mine. Well, different strokes for different folks, you'll say. Really, that's quite kind and understanding of you. But if you ever have the misfortune of actually seeing my feet, which are vaguely reminiscent in both color and shape (I hesitate to say smell, but if truth be

told, sometimes that too) of a sparsely haired underbelly of a dead possum, you'd realize just how extraordinary this man's bedroom behaviors really were. That a person could become so sexually excited -in the full curtain-drawn light of day, no less – by something that I perceived to be so *disgusting* mystified me.

(2013, pp. 60–61)

Our Erotic Template is vibrant and it is a part of ourselves that connects with our sense of aliveness. If we, or someone else, criticise the content of our Erotic Template, it can be extremely shaming and devastating. If someone is courageous enough to share some of their Erotic Template with us, treat them with the utmost care. As part of accepting and embracing our Erotic Template, we can be curious about it and explore it non-judgementally. For example, it is OK to ask ourselves questions about it. For example: "Why does spanking turn me on so much?" There might be a reason, but not always. If there is a reason, the exploration is only to increase our awareness about our Erotic Template, so that we can access better erotic wisdom and choose sexual behaviours according to the erotic wisdom, rather than thinking that it is because we are damaged or weird.

Of course, for some people, there are parts of their Erotic Template that can be problematic, if it contains turn-ons that are illegal. I will explain these in Chapter 9. In this chapter, I am referring to eroticism and turn-ons that are legal and within the context of fantasies and sexual behaviours between consenting adults.

Think about your favourite dessert. Mine is my mother-in-law's homemade apple pie. You can't buy it in shops, the flavours are wonderful and fresh, just the right combination of the morish taste of the apples and the cinnamon. I sometimes eat the apple pie with vanilla ice cream, and sometimes with custard, depending on my mood. I know my mother-in-law makes the apple pie just for me so it makes me feel loved. It is associated with many memories of my mother-in-law surprising me with it; I see her glowing, smiling, loving face when I think of her apple pie. It is also associated with warm memories of family dinners.

Karen's favourite dessert is a carrot cake, with cinnamon icing. It is associated with her favourite season, autumn, when her parents baked them when she was growing up. They served it with a warm cup of tea, while making the house smell of cinnamon with potpourri and scented candles, a tradition she continued in her own home. When she thinks of those moments, her heart fills with warmth and love. Her heart also grieves because her parents passed away and she misses them every autumn.

Paul's favourite dessert is nothing sweet. He prefers a cheese platter accompanied by a glass of very good red wine. He had his first good cheese platter when he went on holiday in France on his honeymoon. He remembers feeling young and a "proper" adult and in love. Although he has divorced since, he has continued to enjoy cheese platters with wine as a special treat for himself.

As you can see, people's favourite desserts are unique, with diverse flavours, associated with specific stories of human connection, emotions, and memories. If someone says, "I love cherry pies", we don't usually question them or think they shouldn't love it. We accept their taste as it is, even if we hate cherry pies. We might even be curious about the stories linked with the cherry pies, but we probably wouldn't feel disgusted by them liking cherry pies. It is the same with our Erotic Template: it is unique, it is associated with specific personal experiences, and it is important for all of us to accept each other's Erotic Template, even if they are very different.

THE FOUR CORNERSTONES OF EROTICISM

The pioneering sexologist Jack Morin (1995) identified common erotic elements that we tend to connect with, which he calls the "four cornerstones of eroticism". My interpretation of these are:

1. *Longing and anticipation.* Some people are erotically stimulated with delayed gratification. They love the sensual and/or romantic anticipation of preparing and planning a sexual encounter. Others are more turned on by longing, which is when people enjoy having their own space away from their lovers so that they can feel the longing and excitement to return to the lovers' space. Some like to tease or be teased, this is a great way to keep the eroticism and sensuality alive in a sexual relationship even when people are not actually having sex in the here-and-now.

2. *Violating prohibition.* As I have discussed in previous chapters, there are so many rules and prohibitions imposed by our society on our sex lives. Whatever sexual orientation people identify with, there are rules about what we should and shouldn't do

with our sex lives. It means that those very prohibitions offer great erotic potency for those who are turned on by being "naughty" or a bit of a rebel in breaking those rules. The more people live within tight prohibitions, the more they are likely to be "naughty". This cornerstone of eroticism can vary greatly depending on the prohibitions that people live with. Women who live in a country that prohibits them from walking in the streets without a man might find walking by themselves very exciting. Women who live in a system that forbids showing any flesh might be turned on by exhibiting their naked legs. In our Western society, common prohibition-breaking behaviours or fantasies that generate eroticism include having multiple partners, having threesomes, being in an open relationship, watching pornography, sex outdoors, sex with toys, men being anally receptive, women being sexually assertive and dominant, same-gender sexual activities, anonymous sex, group sex, sex in sex clubs, paying for sex, spanking, just to name a few. The transgressive is erotic. This cornerstone of eroticism may also be potent in people's fantasies with some prohibitions that they would not wish to act out in real life but nevertheless feel aroused to think about, such as a "gangbang" or unprotected sex. It is because of this cornerstone of eroticism that some people have fantasies that they find disturbing, for example women often report having sexual fantasies of rape. Of course, they don't want it to happen in real life, but allowing themselves to fantasise about it can produce strong eroticism. Heterosexual men often fantasise about having sex with men. It doesn't mean that they are gay and in the closet, but it is this cornerstone of eroticism that is activated. If people fantasise about illegal things, it doesn't mean they are criminals, fantasies are not to be afraid of because they don't necessarily translate into actual behaviours among the general population (Joyal & Carpentier, 2021).

3. *Searching for power.* It is very common for people to feel turned on by an erotic play with power, from very mild to very intense. Making a consensual sexual demand may be erotically powerful, for example, "get on your knees and suck my cock" is often more erotic than "could you please practise fellatio on me, if you don't mind?" Some power play may extend to role plays when one person plays with somebody who has more power than the other. Power play in the context of eroticism is one that can

be embraced in the bedroom but is not translated in the living room, unless people enjoy the Dom/sub lifestyle. Some people want an equal relationship in their everyday lives, but they can play with power in their sex lives within clear established boundaries. Many people who identify as kinky and those in the BDSM community will often find power exchange very erotically potent; for some, it is a dominant colour on their Erotic Template. The fantasies of having sex with a nurse, doctor, police officer, firefighter, boss, or teacher are very common because of this cornerstone of eroticism. For other people, searching for power may simply come with embracing their sexuality fully. For example, men who enjoy their erections may feel powerfully male in that moment. Women who have a fulfilling sex life also report feeling power within their body, mind, and sexuality.

4. *Overcoming ambivalence.* This is basically the awakening of eroticism in a situation that is "hard to get" and finally getting it. It is a less obvious cornerstone because it sometimes intersects with longing and anticipation, violating prohibition, and searching for power, yet it also has its unique potency. Many of us live in the uncomfortable uncertainty of life, and we can feel ambivalence about many areas of our sex lives; "Will they like me?", "Are we going to go on a second date?", "Should we open our relationship to a threesome?", "Should we go to a swingers' club?", "What if it ruins our relationship?", and so on. Thinking about, or venturing into new territories of our sex lives can produce some anxiety. Finally stepping outside of the anxiety and making a decision – overcoming ambivalence – can feel powerfully erotic. For example, deciding to go or not go to a swingers' club may make the people involved in the relationship quite horny. Some people are intensely aroused with sexual behaviours that are risqué (therefore provoking anxiety), for example having sex in their car and getting away with it (not getting caught).

THE TEN TYPES OF EROTIC BOOSTERS

Morin's four cornerstones of eroticism can be thought of as some of the main colours of our Erotic Template. Through years of working with my clients, I have identified some additional elements that can make some of those colours shine brighter at any given time in the here-and-now, which can be entry points to activating our Erotic Template (becoming sexually aroused). I call those the ten types of Erotic Boosters (Neves, 2021).

People can be sexually satisfied with their eroticism when they don't have the booster in their sex lives because it is just that, a boost (the cherry on the cake but not the cake itself). Equally, coming across an Erotic Booster can definitely make people feel sexually aroused, but not necessarily motivated enough to follow through with behaviours. Being aware of our Erotic Boosters means that we can understand the process of our eroticism and sexual arousal on a deeper level and we can also use them to enhance our sex lives as and when we choose.

1. *Visual.* Some people derive much of their erotic boost from what they see. It doesn't make those people "shallow". We all have particular sensitivities to some of our senses. Some people like to see a hairy chest as their erotic boost, some like to look at feet, hair colour, a pair of legs, items of clothing, shoes, tattoos, big breasts, large penis, and so on.

2. *Olfactory.* Some people find smelling particular things sexually arousing. For some, it may be scented candles or flowers. For others, it can be bodily sweat, the smells of a gym, or their partners' skin. For some people, the scent of leather or rubber can be very arousing.

3. *Auditory.* Hearing a lover moan with pleasure can be intensely erotic for some people. They want to hear that their sexual partner is loving how they touch them. Some find sounds that they associate with a sexual atmosphere arousing, for example the sound of club music or jazz. Some like to hear dirty talking throughout their sexual activities. For some people, it could be a particular tone of voice or accent.

4. *Touch.* Some people have an enhanced erotic moment when their body is touched. Typically non-sexual touch can still be erotic, or sensual, for some. For example, we can feel the difference between a hug that is a friendly hug and one that is romantic. Some people love parts of their bodies to be touched that are not the genitals or the body parts that we typically associate with sex, for example, feet, shoulders, neck, ears, thighs. Some people feel erotic potency when there is a skin-to-skin

touch. Others prefer other sensations, like being touched with silk, leather, rubber, feathers, and so on. Some people become aroused only when their genitals are directly stimulated.

5. *Stress.* It may sound strange but some people find stress sexually arousing. Feeling nervous can accelerate the heartbeat, which can also create sexual arousal. For some, it is soothing from stress that is the most potent. For example, when people are in a stressful situation, they might automatically think of sex and feel sexually aroused because they know that sex and orgasms can be a great stress reliever, thus associating stress with sex.

6. *Boredom.* We often hear the story that when there is an electric blackout and therefore nothing to do, people will then have sex (and make babies). This is not such a myth, indeed, as human beings, we tend not to like feeling bored and sex can be a welcome and pleasurable distraction to ward off boredom. It is not in itself an Erotic Booster, but like stress, people can associate boredom with sex if it is their common way to fill up their free, boring time.

7. *Emotional.* Some people are more emotionally driven than others. Some people have an erotic boost when they feel very safe and secure while others tend to feel more sexual if they feel some stress and anxiety. Some feel more sexual when they feel naughty or a low-level anxiety when having anonymous sex, while others need to get to know someone and feel love before they can feel sexually aroused. Some have an erotic boost through anger. It is what is commonly called "make-up sex".

8. *Hormonal.* Some people's Erotic Booster is primarily influenced by their hormones. Men can feel more sexual when they have a testosterone spike, which typically occurs in the morning, while women may have their sexual boost at their ovulating cycle. Of course, it doesn't mean they can't feel sexual at any other time, it just means it might be their best erotic time. Hormones can produce spontaneous sexual desire. The hormonal Erotic Booster is also relevant for people assumed female at birth (AFAB) and assumed male at birth (AMAB) who have gender affirming hormone therapy.

9. *Fantasy.* Some people experience their sexual arousing boost with erotic stories or fantasies. The stories may be through role plays or imagining a particular situation. Some situations may be quite realistic, for example having sex on the kitchen worktop in the middle of cooking, or they can be fantastical, for example having sex on a spaceship on the way to Mars.

10. *Environment.* Most people like having sex in their bedroom because it is an intimate space and it is comfortable. For some people, their erotic boost comes from their space needing to be just right. It could be the bedroom with a specific feature in it, like a mirror, or red velvet curtains, for example. For other people, their erotic boost is in other places, for example the bathroom, the living room, or outside of their own home, like a hotel or a sex club.

These Erotic Boosters are parts of the diverse ways our eroticism gets activated, and how our sex lives can be enhanced, within the full spectrum of human sexual and sensual experiences. It is important to explore those non-judgementally. For example, understanding Erotic Boosters can resolve sexual incompatibility, such as when one person is visually erotically boosted but their partner is touch boosted. One might want sex in front of a mirror and the other might want sex in the dark, under the covers. Understanding the discrepancy in the context of each person's Erotic Template creates space for acceptance and compromise.

Exploring our Erotic Boosters also means that we can be kinder to ourselves and not criticise ourselves too harshly when a spontaneous sexual urge surfaces. Rather than saying "I shouldn't be feeling sexual right now because I'm in the office. It must mean I'm a perv", perhaps we can tell ourselves, "I'm having a moment with my erotic self, it comes and goes. It means I'm human and alive". Some neurodiverse people may have some intense Erotic Boosters as they may be more attuned to certain senses.

THE SOMATIC EROTIC PATHWAYS

In my work, I have also identified other ways that people's eroticism can awaken: through meaningful memories embedded in our Erotic Template, which I call the Somatic Erotic Pathways. These are not necessarily memories that are accessible to our conscious mind such as: "I remember enjoying the position of doggy style, so I'm going to do it again next time". These memories are of a sexual or non-sexual nature that have a sense of deep meaningful connection. They are somatic because the memories do not always have a story or image available in our mind but they usually evoke a sensation in the body instead. Those sensations happen through the pathways of our senses: vision, scent, sound, taste, or touch. I call those memories Erotic Somatic Markers (Neves, 2021). When people come across such markers, they will instantly feel sexual or sensual.

Akemi felt incredibly safe being hugged by her grandfather who wore a particular cologne. When her parents were arguing, she took refuge in her grandfather's arms and smelt his cologne. The scent of his cologne is associated with the sensation of her body being held. Even though there was nothing erotic about her relationship with her grandfather, when she smells the scent of the cologne, she has a sensual reaction in her body, an urge of wanting to be touched and held. The sensual connection was not about her grandfather as an erotic person, but about how meaningful the feelings of safety and protection were for her.

Pierre's first sexual experience with a man was "amazing"; after years of struggling with accepting his sexuality, he finally decided to take the leap and have sex with a man and it was wonderful. That particular man had a goatee beard. Now, years later, happily married to his husband, each time he sees a man with a similar goatee beard, he feels an erotic reaction in his groin area. His Erotic Somatic Marker is not about that man per se, but about the meaningful connection with his sexuality, which does not negate the feelings of love and closeness he has with his husband.

I think it is important to understand such deeper erotic and sensual processes because if we have a sexual urge or sensation erupting, seemingly out of nowhere, we can try to shame ourselves or push it down, instead of embracing it and spending a moment with our feelings. When such urges come, it is not our body telling us that we need to have sex right now, it is telling us it is a moment of meaningful connection with our sensuality, sexuality, and eroticism.

THE EROTIC EQUATION

Jack Morin (1995) came up with The Erotic Equation, a fantastic and simple way to understand how eroticism can operate:

$$\text{Attraction} + \text{Obstacle} = \text{Excitement}$$

The equation shows that if there is something in the way of getting what we want, being with someone, or doing something with someone, then those things become even more exciting. We can see those examples every day:

- The attractive cisgender female attendant smiling at Pete is very exciting because he can't date her as he is in a monogamous marriage with Marie. However, his fantasy of dating her might be very erotic.
- Sandra keeps thinking about her brother's girlfriend, Kate, because she's so attractive, but the very fact that she's out of reach because she's her brother's girlfriend and heterosexual makes wanting her even more exciting.
- Susan thinks she's in love with her boss, Roger; although he is single and available, the fact that she works in a firm where it is inappropriate to date her boss makes wanting him so much more exciting.
- Patrick enjoys watching pornography but his wife hates it and forbids him from watching it, making porn the most exciting forbidden fruit for him.

Sometimes the obstacle may be society's rules, the "should" and "should nots" (a different lens from the cornerstone of eroticism of Violating Prohibition). If the rule is to only ejaculate inside the vagina, ejaculating on someone's breasts or face might be very exciting.

The Erotic Equation explains why dating can be more thrilling than being in a long-term relationship. In dating, we have the initial attraction of the person we are seeing and the uncertainty that the feelings are reciprocated and if there will be further dates with that person. The combination of the attraction and the obstacle makes the dating experience very exhilarating. In contrast, being in a long-term relationship often means that our partner is always available, and the routine makes the relationship less exciting. By the way, it is not a bad thing. Long-term relationships are not supposed to be always super-exciting, it would be exhausting! There are other great benefits to being in a long-term relationship that we can't get in the dating stage. I write more on this in Chapter 8.

Although Morin calls it the Erotic Equation, I would like to call it the "Equation of Desire" because it seems that the same equation can explain how we deeply desire some things that are non-sexual and non-erotic too. As human beings, we don't respond well to deprivation. If the obstacle is a sense of scarcity, we might respond with wanting that thing more, even to levels of obsession sometimes. During the COVID-19 lockdowns, we have observed the "Equation of Desire" in full flow when the mundane satisfaction to have toilet paper became a very exciting object when it became unavailable on the shelves, to the point of obsessing about it, hoarding it, and even having fights about it.

Keeping the Erotic Equation in mind can help us put the puzzle of our Erotic Template together and help make sense of our intense desires and erotic excitement. Knowing that those desires are a normal process of the Erotic Equation can help us be less judgemental about them. Morin writes:

> Some experiences, it seems, are so universal as to be virtually invisible. When the erotic equation restates for people something they already know, they typically react as if a light has pierced the darkness. Suddenly they realize why they're not always attracted to the "right" people, or why the unavailable ones are often the most fascinating.
>
> (1995, p. 50)

EROTIC FANTASIES

I have mentioned fantasies a few times in this chapter so let's dive in deeper now. Many people are afraid of their fantasies, especially those fantasies that may seem unusual, extreme, or even illegal. But we know that fantasies do not necessarily translate into behaviours. Sexual fantasies and sexual behaviours are two very different things that can live side by side in our minds and never collide. Our minds can fantasise a lot. We all do it. We can fantasise about eating a whole chocolate cake and not putting on weight, travelling to Mars, living in a mansion, being James Bond, winning the lottery, and so on. The purpose of fantasies is to give us a respite from the everyday, familiar parts of our lives. They can add some colour to our thinking, bring a smile to our face, titillate us, make us feel alive, and indeed, help us connect with some parts of our erotic mind. We tend not to feel ashamed with non-sexual fantasies. I'm sure we all have spoken openly with our friends about what it would be like to win the lottery, or what we would do if we were the Prime Minister, but when it comes to sexual fantasies, we only dare to have a look at them privately, and, often, with shame. Much of the shame comes from poor sex education and poor understanding of what sexual fantasies actually are. Many fear that they might reveal a dark part of ourselves, but they often don't. Not all sexual fantasies reveal something important about ourselves. The gift of some sexual fantasies is that they can help us go and explore places that are impossible to visit in real life.

Justin Lehmiller (2018) wrote a book *Tell Me What You Want* dedicated to fantasies following his research. Despite the popular belief that only men objectify women, he found that both men and women enjoy objectifying because it's a way to connect with their eroticism. According to Lehmiller's survey, heterosexual women fantasise about men who are taller than average with an athletic body but not too muscly. Women's ideal "fantasy man" has brown or black hair and is more well-endowed than average (2018, p. 132-133). A heterosexual men's "fantasy woman" is also somewhat surprising:

> Straight men in America aren't exactly fantasising about blond bombshells. Instead, most of them are fantasizing about brunette women of average height who have a normal – but not underweight – BMI, are virtually hair-free, and have an ample bosom.
> (2018, p. 135)

Lehmiller found that a lesbian and bisexual women's "fantasy woman" was very similar to a heterosexual man's:

> Strong preference for brunettes over blondes, no body hair, minimal pubic hair and slightly larger than average breasts.
> (2018, p. 136)

Gay and bisexual men also had a similar type of the "fantasy man" to heterosexual women including a preference for athletic bodies over men who are muscle-bound. The only difference is that they are much more particular about the weight of their "fantasy man", which is eight pounds lighter than the heterosexual women's "fantasy man".

Although Lehmiller's research was done with the USA population, I have noticed in my practise that similar types of fantasies are reported with the British and the European populations. We can hypothesise that the fantasies that are so common are partly constructed by the influence of the beauty standard that our Western society prescribes. If we are told enough times that being thin is desirable and beautiful, it becomes unquestionable in our minds. However, some fantasy elements that Lehmiller found go against the popular narrative, for example, that blonde-haired people are more attractive. It is likely that there are multiple sources and influences that make up the fantasies that we find hot, and they are multi-dimensional.

When women objectify it is considered fun because their sexual desire is not perceived as dangerous in our society and therefore it is acceptable and even celebrated on some occasions, like watching the Chippendales' shows for example. A fascinating piece of Lehmiller's research is that he found both men and women fantasise more about their current romantic and sexual partners than famous people or porn stars because we have an emotional bond with our partners. Sexual fantasies are rarely emotionless. It is not correct to think that sexual fantasies are purely sexual (and therefore sleazy). Fantasies have an emotional component, for example the connection with other parts of ourselves such as feeling free of inhibition, imagining being a different lover, and feeling wanted and desired.

Lehmiller also found that the fantasy of public sex showed up very highly in his survey. The public sex fantasy varies from person to person, from sex in an office, toilet cubicle, park, forest, changing rooms, or sex clubs. These type of fantasies are mostly about making sex more exciting by introducing an element of fear or risk (also intersecting with the cornerstone of eroticism of violating prohibition). It doesn't mean that people will have a desire to have sex in public places in their actual lives, but it reflects that we need to inject some naughtiness in order to keep an interest in our erotic lives. Cauliflower with cheese is more enticing than cauliflower on its own, right?

Bering (2013) asserts:

> A lot of human nature has escaped rational understanding because we've been unwilling to be completely honest about what *really* turns us on and off – or at least what's managed to do the trick for us before. We cling to facades.

(2013, p. 23)

We have learnt to be afraid of erotic fantasies because we misunderstand them for sexual reality, and because they are shrouded in shame and taboo due to our pervasive dishonesty about our natural human eroticism.

NOVELTY-SEEKING

As human beings, we are naturally novelty-seeking. It is part of our survival strategy as a species; once we have achieved something, we want to explore something new. This is one of the reasons why we have moved from living in caves to living with the modern technology we have today. Dopamine has a part to play in this, which is why it's a very useful neurotransmitter involved in reward, memory, and learning. We can notice novelty-seeking behaviours in our everyday lives when we open the fridge. We don't want to eat the same dinner every day, it would make for a boring and joyless life. We like to change things up based on the memories of the type of dinners we really love to keep us motivated in feeding ourselves and enjoying life. We search for new recipes that use ingredients we like. Occasionally, we can become very excited by new food we have never tried before or going to a new restaurant for a new experience. Often, we fantasise about food that we can't have in the here and now or in anticipation of food we can have later on in the day. The same novelty-seeking processes happen with our erotic mind. Fantasies and novelty-seeking are good ways to give us a jolt in our erotic mind to remind us to keep in touch with it.

A small minority of people are unable to fantasise. This is part of the phenomenon called aphantasia, which means that they are unable to produce mental images. For most people, if we say "pink elephant" we can pretty much instantly come up with the mental image of the pink elephant. People with aphantasia cannot, therefore it is not possible for them to fantasise. However, they can still be novelty-seeking and have a colourful erotic mind.

FETISH AND KINK

Some people's Erotic Template is dominated by a fetish or kink. Some people may experience their fetish and kink as a leisure activity that they enjoy but don't need to engage with all the time, while other people identify their kink as an erotic orientation, which means that they need to engage with it all the time, or most of the time, in order to find fulfilment in their sex lives.

Sprott and Williams (2019) describe kink and fetish as:

> eroticizing intense sensations (including but not limited to 'pain'), eroticizing power dynamics and power differentials, enduring fascination with specific sensory stimuli including specific body parts or inanimate objects ('fetish'), role play or dramatizing erotic scenarios, and erotic activities that include heightened or altered states of consciousness.

Unfortunately, many people who have a kink or fetish are vulnerable to harsh and shaming criticism for being "weird", "wrong", or "broken" simply because they don't follow the vanilla script that society tells us is normal. For example, people feeling high eroticism with BDSM (bondage, discipline, Dominance, submission, and sadomasochism) are often told they are damaged and there is an assumption that those people interested in BDSM must be reacting to trauma. This assumption is incorrect. Shahbaz and Chirinos (2017) write:

> There is no research that indicates clients with BDSM have a greater history of past abuse or trauma that predisposes them to this form of sexual expression. The practice of BDSM itself does not cause distress and dysfunction in individuals.
>
> (2017, p. 30)

The practice of BDSM rests on the thorough understanding of consent and thus activities are practised with the utmost consciousness. BDSMers have taught the rest of the world about sexual boundaries and consent.

Some fetishes and kinks are considered paraphilias. It is broadly understood that the definition of a paraphilia is a sexual activity or behaviour that falls outside of what is deemed as "normal" or "usual". The word paraphilia is derived from the Greek *para* – meaning beside or aside, and *philos* meaning loving – so the literal translation is "beside/aside loving", generally phrased as "unusual sexual practices". The term paraphilia was included in the Diagnostic and Statistical Manual of Mental Disorders (DSM) in the 1980s to replace the previous problematic terminology of "perversion". The fifth edition of the DSM (APA, DSM-5, 2013) clearly distinguishes paraphilias from paraphilic disorders to emphasise that atypical sexual behaviours are not necessarily pathological. It defines paraphilia as:

> any intense and persistent sexual interest other than sexual interest in genital stimulation or preparatory fondling with phenotypically normal, physically mature, consenting human partners.
>
> (p. 685)

And "paraphilic disorder" as:

> a paraphilia that is currently causing distress or impairment to the individual or a paraphilia whose satisfaction has entailed personal harm, or risk of harm, to others.
>
> (pp. 685–686)

The DSM-5 is clear that the term "diagnosis" for a disorder should be reserved for people who meet both criteria A and B as specified in the manual, meaning that a person has both a paraphilia (criterion A) and negative consequences as a result of the paraphilia (criterion B).

Of course, what is considered a paraphilia may change over time as our perception of what is usual or unusual changes. McManus et al. (2013) point out that the term paraphilia is hard to define in the first place. Moser (2011) criticises the standpoint of what we call "unusual" and questions whether it comes from a heteronormative position rather than a sexological one. Indeed, so many sexual behaviours, desires, or arousals that are considered unusual are so common that one may wonder what "usual" even means. Many so-called unusual behaviours that may fall under the term of paraphilia, for example, voyeurism, is very common, and may not be a problem if the behaviour is done between consenting adults. Like all other sexual behaviours, it becomes a problem when it is non-consensual.

EXPLORING YOUR EROTIC TEMPLATE

Here are some of the central questions you can ask yourself to begin to explore your Erotic Template (Morin, 1995). You can use the same set of questions to help someone else explore their Erotic Template.

Sexual memories

1. Of all the memories of sexual activities and sexual behaviours that you have, select the best one.
2. Why is it the best sexual memory?
3. What are all the big ingredients that make this memory the best?
4. What are all the small little details that make this memory the best?
5. Is this sexual memory associated with a particular sexual activity: kink, BDSM, fetish, vanilla, public sex, group sex, etc.
6. Is this sexual memory associated with particular people?
7. Is this sexual memory associated with a particular place?
8. Is this sexual memory associated with a particular time in your life?
9. Is this sexual memory associated with a particular event? (A celebration, achievement, time of year or season, holidays, weather, etc.)
10. What are the emotions that you remember having at the time when this sexual event took place?
11. What are the emotions that emerge in the here-and-now as you remember this memory?
12. As you remember this memory, do you have a desire to do the behaviour again, or not?
13. Are some of the ingredients present in other sexual memories?
14. Select other sexual memories with similar ingredients and repeat the above process of enquiry. Each response, no matter how small or significant, is a part of your Erotic Template to be aware of and to keep in touch with.

Sexual fantasies

1. Out of all the sexual fantasies that you have, select the best one.
2. Why is it your best sexual fantasy?
3. What are all the big ingredients that make this fantasy the best?
4. What are all the small little details that make this fantasy the best?
5. Is this sexual fantasy associated with a particular sexual activity: kink, BDSM, fetish, vanilla, public sex, group sex, etc.
6. Is this sexual fantasy associated with particular people? (People you know personally, "fantasy" people or celebrities/porn stars.)

7. Is this sexual fantasy associated with a particular place? (Don't forget, it could be a fantastical place like a different planet.)
8. Is this sexual fantasy associated with a particular time in your life? (Including the future.)
9. Is this sexual fantasy associated with a particular event? (A celebration, achievement, time of year or season, holidays, weather, or some fictional events, such as an apocalypse, etc.)
10. What are the emotions that emerge in the here and now as you imagine this fantasy?
11. As you imagine this fantasy, do you have a desire to act on it in reality, or not?
12. Are some of the ingredients present in other sexual fantasies?
13. Select other sexual fantasies with similar ingredients and repeat the above process of enquiry. Each response, no matter how small, significant or fantastical, is a part of your Erotic Template to be aware of and to keep in touch with.

SUMMARY

While we have all heard of gender expressions and sexual orientations, the subject of eroticism is less talked about and certainly less explored. People's eroticism is a vast, rich, and colourful world that is unique to each individual and connected to our sense of self in multiple ways, including how we feel about ourselves and others, what turns us on, what makes us tick, what we fantasise about, and, ultimately what makes us feel alive. Our eroticism intersects with our mental and physical health, the connection with our loved ones, and the very many stories that fill our hearts.

Reflective questions:

1 What have you learnt about your Erotic Template that you knew was there but forgot about it?

2 What have you discovered about your Erotic Template that you didn't know was there?

3 What do you feel about being more in touch with your Erotic Template?

4 What are the "shoulds" and "should nots" you have identified when exploring your fantasies?

5 What are the societal messages you think have got in the way of getting to know your process of eroticism?

6 What can you do to keep in touch with your eroticism as it develops over the year?

FURTHER READING

The Erotic Mind. Unlocking the Inner Sources of Sexual Passion and Fulfillment, by Jack Morin, PhD (1995).

Tell Me What You Want. The Science of Sexual Desire and How It Can Help You Improve Your Sex Life, by Justin Lehmiller, PhD (2018).

Mind The Gap. The Truth About Desire And How To Futureproof Your Sex Life, by Dr Karen Gurney (2020).

REFERENCES

American Psychiatric Association (2013). *Diagnostic and Statistical Manual of Mental Health Disorders*, Fifth Edition (DSM-5). American Psychiatric Publishing. Arlington, VA.

Bering, J. (2013). *Perv, The Sexual Deviant in All of Us*. Penguin Random House UK. London.

Joyal, C., & Carpentier, J. (2021). Concordance and Discordance between Paraphilic Interests and Behaviors: A Follow-Up Study. *The Journal of Sex Research*. doi:10.1080/00224499.2021.1986801

Lehmiller, J. (2018). *Tell Me What You Want. The Science of Sexual Desire and How It Can Help You Improve Your Sex Life*. Robinson. Da Capo Press. New York.

McManus, M.A., Hargreaves, P., Rainbow, L., & Alison, L.J. (2013). Paraphilias: Definition, Diagnosis and Treatment. *F1000prime Reports*, 5, 36. doi:10.12703/P5-36

Morin, J. (1995). *The Erotic Mind. Unlocking the Inner Sources of Sexual Passion and Fulfillment*. HarperCollins. New York.

Moser C. (2011). Yet another Paraphilia Definition Fails. *Archives of Sexual Behavior*, 40, 483–485. doi:10.1007/s10508-010-9717-x.

Neves, S. (2021). *Compulsive Sexual Behaviours. A Psycho-Sexual Treatment Guide for Clinicians*. Routledge. Abingdon, Oxon.

Shahbaz, C., & Chirinos, P. (2017). *Becoming a Kink Aware Therapist*. Routledge. New York.

Sprott, R.A., & Williams, D.J. (2019). Is BDSM a Sexual Orientation or Serious Leisure? *Current Sexual Health Reports*, 11, 75–79. doi:10.1007/s11930-019-00195-x

THE BASIC PHYSIOLOGY OF SEX

The physiology of sex is the more "technical" aspect of sexology and perhaps the most difficult to understand if you're not a medical professional. But don't worry, neither am I, so I'm going to make it simple. However, it is an integral part of sexology so it is important to know about it. One of the main focuses of clinical sexology is to investigate what is functional and what is not, what are the causes of the sexual issues people have, and how to treat them. Another goal of the profession is to help people enhance their sex lives and levels of sexual pleasure. In order to do so, we need a good understanding of the biology of the parts of our bodies that are involved with our sex lives: our genitals and our brain.

THE ANATOMY OF PEOPLE ASSIGNED OR ASSUMED FEMALE AT BIRTH (AFAB)

The clitoris

The clitoris has been notoriously poorly examined and understood over many decades, this is perhaps because most of the people in charge of sexual health research were men. Many doctors today still have a poor understanding of the clitoris. It is only in recent years with the technological advancement of MRI that we have begun to understand it much better. Guess what we found? The clitoris is a very special and unique organ. Its sole purpose is sexual pleasure. Yes, that's right. There aren't any other body parts that have the sole purpose of sexual pleasure. None.

DOI: 10.4324/9781003276913-6

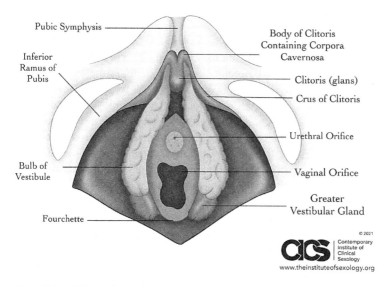

Figure 5.1   Clitoris. Reproduced with permission from CICS.

Structurally, the clitoris is like an inverted "Y" – the tip is folded and it has two sets of arms. The tip is known as the glans and is partially covered by the clitoral hood.

The clitoris is not only the glans (what is seen externally), it has an internal structure too. The clitoris sits on top of the urethra, its arms draped over each side. One set of arms (3 to 7 centimetres in length) sits next to the urethra, the others (5 to 9 centimetres in length) are roughly beneath the labia majora. Sexologists describe this structure as "clitorourethrovaginal complex", a bit of a mouthful.

It is not just the glans that is sensitive to sexual pleasure, all parts of the clitoris are erectile and involved in sexual pleasure. Moreover, the part of the brain that receives the touch signals from the clitoris overlaps with the part that is connected to receiving touch signals from nipples, which means that a touch on one part of the body evokes a pleasure response on another part of the body. It also means that a person who has had part of the clitoris removed or damaged can still orgasm.

Vulva and vagina

These two areas are also poorly understood. People use the words vulva and vagina interchangeably but they are two different things. The vulva is the external part of the genitals and the vagina is the internal part. Unlike the penis, it is hard for people with vulvas to easily look at them, it takes a mirror to have a proper look. Many people don't spend any time trying to get to know their vulva and it somehow feels like a body part that they don't own. There is very poor sex education about the genitals of AFAB people and even physicians are not very good at giving the right information. Accurate education is crucial because the lack of knowledge of their anatomy means that AFAB people can't make informed consent, or explain where they may have a problem to their healthcare professionals if they don't understand their bodies properly.

Historically, the vulva and the vagina were subject to terrible thinking. In the 1920s and 30s, physicians believed that vaginas were filled with dangerous bacteria. At the time, there were no physicians with vaginas so everything doctors learnt about the vagina was interpreted as they wished. The world of medicine was full of "mansplaining"! The narrative of the "dirty vagina" prevails today, encouraged by many products being sold on the market for vaginal cleansing and scented vaginal products.

The truth is, the vagina is protected by good bacteria that fight off infections from urine and faeces. It heals very well after childbirth. The whole structure is a wonderful design of nature to withstand and protect itself against a lot of things that can happen in that region of the body.

The labia and the mons

These exist to enhance sexual pleasure and to protect the opening of the vagina. The mons is the area of skin and fatty tissue from the pubic bone down to the clitoral hood. The labia majora are folds of hair-bearing skin and fatty tissues – filled with glands. The labia minora have no fat but have erectile tissue that swells in response to arousal. Suction or pull on the labia minora stimulates the clitoris so they have a sexual function. They have specific nerve endings important for sexual response, especially along their edge. They are capable of distinguishing touch on a very fine scale.

Some people with vulvas may feel bad about their labia because they may think they don't look "right", meaning it doesn't look like

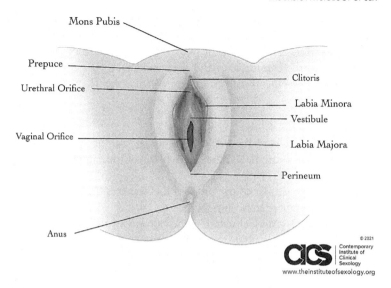

Mons Pubis

Prepuce

Clitoris

Urethral Orifice

Labia Minora

Vestibule

Vaginal Orifice

Labia Majora

Perineum

Anus

© 2021

Contemporary
Institute of
Clinical
Sexology
www.theinstituteofsexology.org

Figure 5.2   Vulva. Reproduced with permission from CICS.

the only version that we may have been exposed to in erotic media and pornography. It is important to know that there is no normal size or shape of the labia minora. They may or may not protrude beyond the labia majora, and both labia majora and minora may not be symmetrical. In sexology, we say that both set of labia are "sisters", not "twins". Vulvas all look different; like faces, they have the same parts in slightly different dimensions.

The vulva skin and pubic hair

Under a microscope, all skin looks like a brick wall with cells layered on top of each other, each layer moves upwards to the surface to keep regenerating the skin. As the cells move upwards to the outer layer, they produce a protein called keratin that is waterproof and helps the cells resist injury. At the surface, the skin cells release fatty substances to protect against trauma and injury and to trap moisture. The top layer of cells are dead and brush off – a new layer is replaced every 30 days or so.

The mons and labia majora have eccrine glands to secrete perspiration and pheromones important in sexual attraction and arousal.

Each pubic hair is attached to a nerve ending – so tugging can produce sexual pleasure. The pubic hair traps moisture and pheromones. The glands producing these substances don't develop until puberty. It is hypothesised, therefore, that this smell is part of sexual attraction. The shaving of pubic hair, which is very popular, can produce micro-trauma to the skin and make this area of the body more vulnerable to infection.

The vestibule

The vestibule is where the vulva becomes the vagina. The urethra is located in the vestibule. There are two sets of specialised glands:

Skene's glands: similar to the prostate that secretes tiny amounts of PSA (prostate specific antigen).
The Bartholin's glands: situated at the bottom of the vestibule, on either side, contribute a small amount of lubrication (they sometimes become blocked and form painful cysts).

The anus

The anus is another body part that is taboo, we don't talk much about it, especially regarding sexual pleasure. The anus has two muscular rings, an internal and external one, called sphincters.

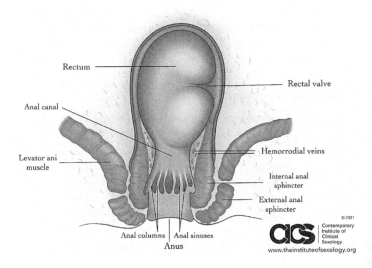

Figure 5.3   Anus. Reproduced with permission from CICS.

The lining of the anus is packed full of nerve endings to allow us to distinguish between fluid, faeces, and gas, and to help us coordinate the socially acceptable time for emptying.

The abundance of nerves is why the anus is very sensitive, and anal stimulation can produce much sexual pleasure. It is also why issues with the anus, like tears, and piles, hurt so much.

A closer look at the vagina

The hymen used to be thought of as a marker of whether a person is a virgin or not. In the foetus, the vagina is a closed tube that gradually opens from the inside out. The hymen is usually broken a long time before the first occurrence of sexual intercourse. Any remaining remnants of the closure of the hymen often break prior to the first intercourse due to tampons or exercise. The ghastly "virginity test" is shaming, sex-negative, and cannot be accurate.

The vagina is lined with specialised skin called mucosa, arranged in folds called rugae. This sits on top of a layer of smooth muscle: it is believed this helps move blood or discharge to the vaginal opening.

The smooth muscle is surrounded by a rich network of blood vessels, this is why the vagina heals so well after injury (or childbirth).

The vagina gets wider inside moving towards the cervix. The vaginal length varies significantly, a person's body size and shape don't predict this, just the same as a person's height (or shoe size) doesn't predict the size of the penis.

The vagina extends in length when aroused, which is why inserting a tampon (when not aroused) feels different to inserting a penis or a sex toy when aroused.

The pelvic floor muscles

The pelvic floor muscles are two layers of muscle that wrap around the vagina for structural support. They assist with continence and are arranged like a hammock with the three "exits" of the vagina, urethra, and rectum passing through.

The pelvic floor muscles contract between three to fifteen times during orgasm. They are typically not under conscious control. If those muscles are too weak prolapses can happen, if they are too tight they can cause sexual or pelvic pain.

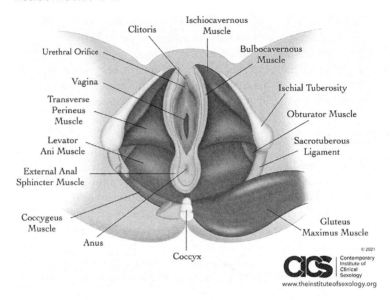

Figure 5.4   AFAB Pelvic Floor Muscles. Reproduced with permission from CICS.

The vaginal mucosa

The lining of the vagina – in the fertile years – is about 28 cell layers thick. They have less keratin, meaning they are not waterproof but slightly leaky. This leakage is called transudate. When a person is aroused, the blood flow to the vagina suddenly increases a lot, creating much more leakage. We call it getting "wet". Trans women with a neo-vagina don't lubricate in the same way.

The vaginal mucosa turns over much faster than vulval skin, with a new surface layer every 96 hours. This is to repair it from sex, to feed the bacteria that keep the vagina healthy, and to reduce the bad bacteria that can cause infection.

Discharge is healthy and normal. The typical vagina produced 1–3 ml daily, but up to 4 ml is normal (that's enough to completely soak a mini pad).

One of the main bacterial species in the vagina is lactobacillus. They protect the vagina and keep the pH between 3.5–4.5 which makes it hard for other bad bacteria to thrive. It basically acts like a homemade antibiotic!

Vaginal pH increases during periods, the blood binds lactobacilli. This is why some people can get thrush at the end of their periods.

After menopause, the cell lining gets two-thirds thinner and the pH increases. This can cause significant problems for some people.

The internal reproductive system of AFAB people

This is a brief description of the different parts of the reproductive system of cisgender women and most AFAB people. Some people with vulvas, including trans women and some intersex people may have a different system. Some cisgender women who had a medical procedure such as a hysterectomy to treat an illness (cancer, for example) won't have a reproductive system.

> *Uterus (womb).* The main function of the uterus is to house the baby while it grows and to push the baby during vaginal childbirth.
>
> *Cervix.* A doughnut shaped body connects the vagina and the uterus. It has an inner and outer "O" – or opening. It dilates to 10 cm during vaginal childbirth.

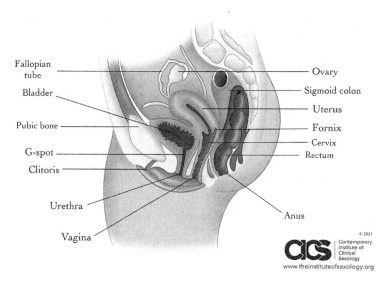

Figure 5.5   AFAB Reproductive System. Reproduced with permission from CICS.

Uterine isthmus. The thinnest and lowest section of the uterus.
Corpus. The main body of the uterus.
Fundus. The topmost section of the uterus.
The walls of the corpus and fundus have three layers:

> *Perimetrium*: Tough outer layer of connective tissue (supports the uterus).
> *Myometrium*: Muscular layer responsible for contracting during labour.
> *Endometrium*: Blood vessel rich innermost layer, thickens under hormonal influence every month, prepares for possible conception and pregnancy. The painful condition endometriosis is where this tissue grows elsewhere in the pelvis due to retrograde menstruation and can cause severe pain and adhesions between other internal organs.

Fallopian tubes. Tiny, muscular tubes 8–14 cm long, that end in fimbriae which sit close to the ovaries and guide the ova (egg) released at ovulation into the tubes.

Ovaries. Located on either side of the uterus. Produces oestrogen, progesterone, and some testosterone (the sex hormones), under the influence of the pituitary gland in the brain.

Menstrual cycle: they normally happen every 21–35 days; a cycle of hormonal activity leading to the release of a mature ova (egg), and the eventual shedding of the newly thickened endometrium (womb lining), if the ova isn't fertilised.

Menstruation: this is the medical term for a period. It is the loss of blood, tissue, and other debris from the uterus as the inner lining sheds. The blood flow on average can last between four and six days. It has an impact on iron levels and can contribute to anaemia. Not all people who identify as women have periods and not all people who have periods identify as women.

The sexual response in AFAB people

There are different models that attempt to understand sexual response, some of which come with controversies and debate. The classic model of sexual response was first presented by Masters and Johnson (1966). It focused on physical changes of arousal. The

Masters and Johnson's four-phase model is: (1) excitement, (2) plateau, (3) orgasm, (4) resolution. This model has been criticised for not including desire (if you dislike your partner or they turn you off, getting aroused can be a challenge).

Helen Singer Kaplan (1974) added desire to Masters and Johnson's Four-Phase Model and divided these into a psychological phase and a physiological phase:

1. Psychological phase: sexual desire before excitement.
2. Physiological phase: excitement and orgasm.

Both these models are based on the assumption that there is a pre-existing specific sexual desire. They neglect the other reasons that many women, and men, and people of other genders, report for wanting sexual intimacy, like emotional connection, trust, and affection.

Kleinplatz (Kaschak & Tiefer, 2001) challenges the male-centric sexological knowledge with a feminist perspective:

> Changes in women's bodies are seen as dangerous, volatile, evidence of instability and unpredictability, in need of control – not something to delight and revel in and to experience as an entry point to profound, erotic joy … The role of this reductionistic, clinical view in denying female sexuality is readily illustrated by examining our views of pregnancy, childbirth and breastfeeding. Our society in general and both medical and mental health professions tend to medicalize and simultaneously de-sexualise these events.
>
> (2001, p. 127)

Rosemary Basson (2001) presents a more modern model because it is a non-linear one. Basson created a circular model that puts more emphasis on the importance of multi-dimensional factors in seeking out and being receptive to sexual response in women including: emotional intimacy, sexual stimuli, sexual arousal, arousal and sexual desire, emotional and physical satisfaction, spontaneous sexual drive.

Emily Nagoski (2015) reminds us of the dual control model developed by Janssen and Bancroft in the late 1990s: (1) sexual excitation system, (2) sexual inhibition system. The excitation system is the accelerator of our sexual response and the inhibition system is our brakes. Nagoski argues that the dual control model is useful in helping us understand our turn-ons and turn-offs and therefore how to make changes for an optimal sex life:

> you can immediately conceptualize all sexual functioning – and all sexual dysfunction – as a balance (or imbalance) between brakes and accelerator. If you're having trouble with any phase of sexual response, is it because there's not enough stimulation to the accelerator? Or is there too much stimulation to the brakes? Indeed, a common mistake made by people who are struggling with orgasm or desire is assuming that the problem is a lack of accelerator; it's more likely that the problem is too much brake.
>
> (2015, p. 50)

Conditions for good sex

Dr Karen Gurney (2020) offers her model for the conditions for good sex:

- Psychological arousal
- Physical touch
- Being in the moment

These three conditions need to be present, and they interact with each other, which means that good sex can be a fine balance. Gurney explains:

> distraction reduces our ability to experience sexual sensation. Being more turned on makes it more likely that we are absorbed in the moment. High levels of psychological arousal are great, but not if the touch is unpleasant, as then it will decline. High levels of psychological arousal and our preferred physical touch will have no impact if all we can focus on is what our thighs look like or whether the other person is thinking of their ex.
>
> (2020, p. 65)

Desire and arousal

However it is described, sexual arousal in humans encompasses a mental state (emotional and cognitive) and a physical state induced by various stimuli (touch, smell, sounds, or any Erotic Boosters) that usually produce feelings of pleasure and initiate a desire to continue the activity, often to orgasm.

General physical characteristics of arousal in the body of most people with vulvas, which extend to the brink of orgasm, include the following:

1. The vagina swells from increased blood flow, turning the vaginal walls to a dark purple and increasing transudate (wetness).
2. The clitoris engorges with blood, becoming highly sensitive (may even be painful to touch) and retracts under the clitoral hood to avoid direct stimulation.
3. Breathing, heart rate, and blood pressure increase.
4. Muscle spasms may begin in the feet, face, and hands.
5. Tension in the muscles increases.
6. The lower third of the vagina can tighten a little due to swelling, as well as the tightening of the pubococcygeous muscle, forming the "orgasmic platform".
7. The upper two-thirds of the vagina can dilate significantly.
8. The uterus lifts up.
9. The nipples harden and the breasts swell.

Non-concordance in sexual response

It is more common in the response of people with vulvas than people with penises (but possible in all, including people with a prostate). Those physical changes in arousal are mediated by a sacrospinous reflex, which means they can happen without subjective arousal. Mental arousal (or fantasies) can occur without physical changes in the genitals, and physical changes can occur without mental arousal. This is why many people with vulvas and/or prostates may experience sexual arousal or pleasure responses even when the sexual contact is unwanted. When it happens, it confuses people a lot, leading to blaming themselves for it ("if I felt aroused, it must mean I wanted it").

Many parts of the human body can evoke arousal when caressed – though the most sensitive structures usually lie in and around the genitalia. Those parts of the body can be stimulated by different means: vibrators, dildos, fingers, orally, as well as by penetration.

Orgasm

Orgasms are not under conscious control. Once the body reaches orgasm, it does what it needs to do by itself. The orgasmic muscle platform contracts rhythmically three to 15 times. The contractions typically last for five to 60 seconds. The uterus contracts too, as well as the anal sphincter.

Orgasms usually create a feeling of well-being and relaxation. The hormone oxytocin is released, causing feelings of closeness and bonding.

Resolution phase

After the orgasm, the clitoris descends and the blood engorgement subsides. The labia return to their unaroused colour and size. The uterus descends to the unaroused position. The vagina shortens and narrows back to its unaroused state. People with vulvas have no refractory period (the time between an orgasm and when a person feels ready to be sexually aroused again), so multiple orgasms are possible.

The myths of the orgasm of people with vulvas

The orgasm is somewhat a topic that people love to talk about. There are three prevalent myths that are often spread on this subject: the "vaginal orgasm", the "G-spot", and "squirting".

Vaginal orgasms

Many people believe that vaginal orgasms are different from clitoral orgasms and that, somehow, vaginal orgasms are something to aspire to. The reality is that all orgasms are clitoral. Only a small minority of people with vulvas are capable of achieving orgasm with penile penetration alone. Reaching orgasm through clitoral stimulation is the norm in solo and partnered sex. It is thought that there are more than 8,000 nerve endings in the glans of the clitoris alone – that's double the number in the penis!

The G-spot

The famous G-spot was first identified by Ernst Gräfenberg (1950) – though he actually called his scientific paper *The Role of the Urethra in Female Orgasm*. Gräfenberg was referring to the more sensitive anterior wall of the vagina, just in front of the urethra (he missed the clitoris). What we might refer to today as the G-spot is actually one of the arms of the clitoris.

The terms vaginal orgasm and the G-spot are not helpful because the clitoris is the usual route towards orgasm. As I have explained earlier, the clitoris is a much bigger structure than what is visible, so it is stimulated in many ways.

Squirting

Yes, women can ejaculate, but not in as impressive a way as it is shown in pornography. Skene's glands typically release about 1–2 ml of "ejaculate" (in contrast, people with penises and testes release about 5 ml of semen). Some people with vulvas can experience what is called "a big gush" of ejaculate (it is sometimes made up with urine), but because the "big gush" is possible for some women, it doesn't mean that it is the "gold standard" or the hallmark of the "best orgasm". Some people squirt more than others, but there should not be any pressure to achieve squirting.

Childbirth

Childbirth is often discussed as an amazing thing, but the reality is that it is not always a joyous experience. It's often a leap of faith, full of uncertainty and the unknown, and quite an anxiety-inducing experience. The positive experience of childbirth depends on the birthing person's social network, circumstances, and how they discovered their pregnancy. For example, Monica's partner immediately left her as soon as he discovered her pregnancy. Her emotions during childbirth were a mixture of sadness, anger, and shame for "not giving a father to her newborn baby". Adisa could not get pregnant easily. After months and months of failed attempts, she finally became pregnant and both she and her husband were excited. Her childbirth was filled with joy and gratitude. Niamh chose to have a baby by herself through sperm donation. Her family was morally against her having a child without being married. Her parents told her they did not want to speak to her or meet her baby. Her childbirth was a mix of joy for doing what she had always wanted to do, as well as sadness and loneliness for being abandoned by her family.

The body of AFAB people with an internal reproductive system is designed to give birth, yet that doesn't mean childbirth goes smoothly. It is a complicated process. Before childbirth actually occurs, a pregnant person will feel contractions, hours, days, or sometimes weeks before childbirth. These are called Braxton-Hicks contractions. The uterus makes periodic movements of contraction and release to prepare for labour. The contractions will become more frequent as the time of birth approaches. The baby will move further down the pelvis, head first, close to the cervix. The cervix dilates so that the baby can eventually enter the vagina. Just before labour, the membrane containing the baby breaks releasing fluids out of the vagina, which is typically called "breaking waters". By then, a birthing person should be supported by a midwife or doula to help the safe delivery of the baby. In Western countries, the health of a birthing person is carefully monitored at each step of the way from the moment of the discovery of pregnancy. There may be complications that can be foreseen, and in some circumstances having a baby by caesarean, which is a surgical procedure to deliver a baby through the abdomen, may be recommended.

Hormonal changes in pregnancy

The endocrinology of pregnancy is complex and facilitates huge metabolic changes. Human chorionic gonadotrophin (hCG) is only produced during pregnancy, in large amounts in the placenta. It may be responsible for pregnancy nausea and vomiting. Human placental lactogen (hPL) is produced in the placenta; it supplies the foetus with nutrition and develops breasts for milk production.

Progesterone is vital to suppress immunological responses that would reject the foetus and maintain pregnancy. It is also necessary to allow relaxation of major anatomical structures and increase blood flow to the uterus. It can also be the cause of constipation, wind, and bloating during pregnancy. Later in the pregnancy, progesterone strengthens the pelvic floor ready for the mechanisms of labour.

Oestrogen is produced to allow the growth of major vessels and placental health. It also enables foetal organs to develop. It prepares the uterus for labour and the breasts for breastfeeding. However, the increased production of oestrogen will cause softening of major ligaments and muscle groups so backache and discomfort can occur. Common symptoms of the early pregnancy (first trimester) are:

1. Mood swings.
2. Tiredness and lethargy.
3. Nausea and vomiting.
4. Tearfulness.
5. Lack of libido.
6. Anxiety, and being worried about the baby.

In mid-pregnancy (second trimester), the common symptoms are:

1. Having more energy.
2. Lustrous skin and hair.
3. There are noticeable changes to the body.
4. Breasts enlarge.
5. Increase or return of libido.
6. Feeling happy for the ongoing pregnancy.

In late pregnancy (third trimester), the typical symptoms are:

1. Increased body mass.
2. The foetus is fully developed.
3. The placenta is fully developed.
4. The pelvic floor is under duress.
5. The rectum and bladder are unable to hold contents as easily.
6. Tiredness returns.
7. Feeling more emotionally up and down and agitated.
8. Less likely to want sex.

Lochia

Lochia is the vaginal discharge following childbirth. It contains blood, mucous, and shedding tissue from the uterus. The discharge lasts for approximately four to six weeks.

There are three phases of lochia:

1. Lochia rubra (bright red).
2. Lochia serosa (paler, pink).
3. Lochia alba (creamy discharge).

Changes in the amount of discharge, colour, or odour could signify an infection or other complication.

Breasts and breastfeeding

Very early in pregnancy the changes that are necessary for breast-feeding occur. There are visible changes to the nipples, they become darker and more erect, and the breasts grow. They may leak from the second trimester onwards. In the postpartum period, breasts are swollen and tender due to lactation factors.

Post-birth psychological well-being

There is a significant (and normal) fluctuation of hormones post-birth, which means that most birthing people are tearful in the first few weeks postpartum. However, the combination of low mood together with poor quality sleep and fluctuating hormones can lead to postnatal depression and all birthing people are monitored for this in the first six weeks after birth by healthcare professionals. Anxiety is also a common psychological issue throughout and after pregnancy, and in some cases, obsessive compulsive disorder (also known as "OCD"). In the UK, there are perinatal mental health teams attached to each hospital to help support people during and after pregnancy.

If the birth did not happen as expected, it is possible that the birthing person, as well as their partner(s), experience it as a birth trauma, and may be affected by post-trauma stress. A study by Leeds and Hargreaves (2008) found that perceptions of childbirth experiences contribute to the levels of distress after birth. For example, a fear of physical harm or death to themselves or the baby, and the loss of control precipitates the development of post-traumatic stress disorder (PTSD) after childbirth. Notably, there is a high level of PTSD reported when the birth involved an unexpected emergency procedure. In these cases, birthing people may be left with a sense of self-defectiveness, blaming themselves for letting down their baby or "not doing birth properly".

Menopause

Menopause describes "the last period". It is only a diagnosis that can be made retrospectively after 12 months of no periods. Everything before this time is termed perimenopause and everything after this time is termed post-menopause.

People experience menopause in many different ways, so, again, there is no "normal". However, it is useful to know what the "usual" menopause looks like.

The average age for the usual menopause is around 50–51. It is a gradual process that has an impact physiologically, socially, and psychologically. The periods can change in different ways. For some people, they may get heavier or even lighter, and they may also occur more often or for others more spaced out. This whole process can take up to four to seven years but can be longer in some people.

Some people may experience what is called early menopause when it happens between 40 to 45 years of age. For some people whose menopause starts below the age of 40, it is termed premature ovarian insufficiency (POI). Some trans men who take testosterone for their gender affirming process may experience early menopause. Some menopauses are induced surgically if there is a medical need to remove ovaries. The menopause then may be experienced as abrupt and severe. Breast cancer patients may also experience a sudden onset of menopause with severe symptoms due to the effects of their medical treatment.

Symptoms of menopause

Not all people know if they are in perimenopause or menopause. Typically, there are symptoms for a long time prior to menopause, including:

1. Vasomotor symptoms.
2. Psychological symptoms.
3. Genital and sexual symptoms.
4. Skin and joint symptoms.

The most common vasomotor symptom is what we call hot flushes: sensations of heat or sweating (or both), usually in the face and upper torso, during the daytime, nighttime, or both. These symptoms occur because the change in levels of oestrogen significantly narrows the zone of the body's temperature control. Exercise, hot drinks, stress, and anxiety all create more hot flushes. Cortisol (the stress hormone) makes hot flushes worse. Worrying about the flushes can create more stress, leading to more hot flushes. Many people are trapped in this vicious cycle.

Other vasomotor symptoms include palpitations, feeling dizzy or faint, increased migraines, and feelings of pressure in the face or head.

The common psychological symptoms of menopause are:

1. Feeling tense or nervous.
2. Insomnia (not just being woken by hot flushes).
3. Feeling excitable or agitated.
4. Difficulty concentrating ("brain fog").
5. Forgetfulness.
6. Feeling tired.
7. Feeling low and unhappy.
8. Crying more easily.
9. Feeling irritable.
10. Feeling less able to cope with things.

There are also common genitourinary and sexual symptoms. Oestrogen keeps the reproductive organs healthy when people are fertile. After menopause, the lining of the vagina and urinary tracts thins significantly, and it is often harder to fight off urinary tract infections, lubricate for sex, feel sexual touch as intensely or pleasurable as before, or "stretch" to accommodate sex as comfortable as before, and they may experience a loss of libido. The blood flow to the pelvic floor muscles and organs reduces so they get weaker, which makes continence and prolapse issues more likely.

Muscles, bones, and skin are also affected by the menopause. Oestrogen is vital for normal collagen production and bone health.

Bone density falls significantly during the perimenopause and then continues at a slower pace after the menopause, increasing osteoporosis and fracture risk. People going through the menopause may also experience other common symptoms such as joint aches, muscle pains and stiffness, numbness or tingling in hands and feet, and skin itching and dryness.

The duration of menopause symptoms can last a long time, but it varies greatly. Some people report symptoms lasting two to three years, while others have symptoms lasting for seven years or more.

The most common treatment to alleviate the menopause symptoms is hormone replacement therapy (HRT). It is important that people consult with their doctors about it for an individualised treatment plan because HRT may not always be recommended. Often, the decision to embark on HRT is to balance the risk of the treatment (small risk of breast cancer) and the improvement of the quality of life that it may bring.

HRT is composed of oestrogen and progesterone. These hormones can come in synthetic or body identical formulations and in different doses. There are different routes of delivery such as oral tablets, transdermal, or via implants. Doctors can help people decide which HRT will be best for an individual. People who have had a hysterectomy can have oestrogen on its own. All other people must have progesterone in some form as well to protect the womb lining.

There are some clear contra-indications for HRT. People who should never have HRT are:

1. Those who had an oestrogen-dependent cancer (past or current).
2. Those with undiagnosed vaginal bleeding (bleeding after sex, or sudden change in pattern).
3. Those who are pregnant.
4. Those with active liver disease with abnormal blood tests.
5. Those who currently have blood clots, or have had a recent heart attack.

HRT has received a bad press and it is a controversial topic, however the medical evidence is clear that HRT is the most effective treatment for menopause symptoms as well as being recommended by NICE (National Institute for Health and Care Excellence). Of course, the treatment is not without risks, so it is important to discuss the risks as well as the benefits of HRT with a medical professional.

THE ANATOMY OF PEOPLE ASSIGNED OR ASSUMED MALE AT BIRTH (AMAB)

Penis

The penis is composed of the glans and shaft. It has the dual role of sex and urination, as it contains the urethra too.

The shaft of the penis has three cylinders of spongy erectile tissue: two cylinders called corpora cavernosa, and one cylinder called corpus spongiosum, which contains the urethra.

The size of penises varies greatly.

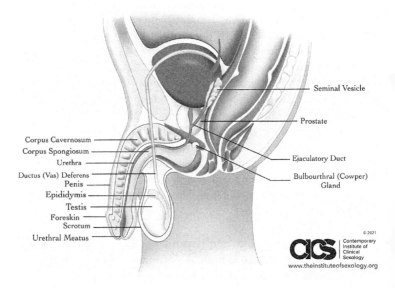

Figure 5.6   AMAB Anatomy. Reproduced with permission from CICS.

Scrotum and testes

The scrotum contains the testes. They are in an external sac for temperature control because the optimal temperature for sperm is slightly lower than body temperature.

The testes are two oval organs about the size of table tennis balls. They are secured in the scrotum by a structure called the spermatic cord. The testes produce testosterone, what is called the primary "male sex hormone". They also make sperm.

Epididymis

The epididymis is the long, coiled tube resting on the back of each testicle. It transports and stores sperm cells that are produced in the testes. It also brings the sperm to maturity, since the sperm that emerge from the testes are immature and incapable of fertilization. During sexual arousal, contractions of the tube eject the sperm into the vas deferens.

Vas deferens

The vas deferens is the long muscular tube that passes from the epididymis into the pelvic cavity, joins the urethra and transports the mature sperm to the urethra.

The ejaculatory ducts

The ejaculatory ducts are formed by the fusion of the vas deferens and the seminal vesicles which empty into the urethra.

The pelvic floor muscles

The pelvic floor muscles are involved in orgasm, emission, and expulsion during ejaculation.

The anus

As mentioned earlier, the anus is full of nerve endings and it is therefore sensitive to touch. Unlike the vagina, the anus does not lubricate in response to sexual stimuli but its close proximity to the prostate means that anal penetration can stimulate it which is intensely pleasurable for some people. The anus has delicate tissues and a high blood supply so there is a higher likelihood of sexually transmitted infections (STI) through anal sex.

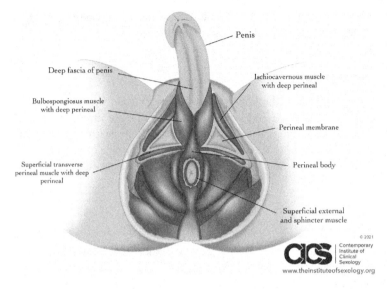

Figure 5.7   AMAB Pelvic Floor Muscles. Reproduced with permission from CICS.

The sexual response in AMAB people

The various models discussed in the sexual response in AFAB people may also apply with AMAB people: Masters and Johnson's four-phase model, Singer-Kaplan's psychological/physiological model, Basson's circular model, the dual control model and Gurney's conditions of good sex.

Erection

An erection is a complex process. It involves good communication between the brain and the genitals, blood flow, and hormones. It needs both a positive psychological disposition as well as good reflex factors. A satisfactory balance of these leads to erections.

The brain has two main "erection centres":

1. A cluster of neurons in the medial preoptic area (MPOA), inside the hypothalamus (the part of the brain that produces hormones), triggers an erection.

2. The paraventricular nucleus also sends and receives messages from other areas of the brain and spinal cord. It releases oxytocin, a powerful pro-erectile hormone.

The penis has two chambers of spongy tissues, the corpora cavernosa. During an erection, the blood flows into the penile arteries and fill the corpora cavernosa with blood. The penile veins get compressed by swelling of the corpora, trapping the blood in the penis. The erection ends when the brain stops sending signals that indicate sexual arousal: the hormonal response ends, the veins and arteries go back to normal, and the penis returns to a soft state.

It means that erections are controlled cerebrally:

1. Caused by erotic images, visual stimuli, or thoughts.
2. The main brain structure involved in erections is in the hypothalamus.
3. Dopamine is the most important brain neurotransmitter for erection, stimulated by oxytocin release.
4. The autonomic nervous system (the system that controls and regulates our bodily functions without our conscious control) is the baseline for sexual function and erections: the parasympathetic system (when the nervous system is in a calm state) is the main mediator for erections.

Erections are, therefore, a neurovascular event: teamwork between blood vessels and nerves. The sexual response requires a balance between "brakes" and "accelerators". The brakes are in inhibitory input from the sympathetic nervous system (the fight or flight system) and the excitatory input of the parasympathetic system (calm, rest, and digest). It is a fine balance. If there is too much calm, there might not be enough good stress for sexual arousal (e.g. the heart beating faster), but if there is too much stress, the system flips into fight or flight where the blood flows away from the penis and into the other parts of the body needed for flight or fight (because erections don't happen when the body is in the "threat" mode).

Many people want to have good erections but they may experience a lot of anxiety about their ability to be a good lover, or the fear of not having an erection. That fear and anxiety trigger the sympathetic system (fight or flight), which is counter-erections, and the very anxiety of not having an erection makes the fear come true.

Reflex erections

The reflex erections don't involve erotic thoughts or images in the brain. They occur in the erection-generating centre of the spinal cord. They are thought to happen to keep erectile tissue healthy, by flushing it with blood. This is why people experience night-time erections.

Orgasm

An orgasm is a powerful and highly pleasurable pelvic muscle contraction. It usually happens at the same time as ejaculation, but ejaculation and orgasm are not the same things as they are two different body processes. Following orgasm, people with penises (unlike people with vulvas) will have a temporary period of inhibition of erection or ejaculation called the refractory period. The length of the refractory period varies greatly.

Ejaculation

Ejaculation is controlled by the autonomic nervous system (the system that is outside our conscious control) and has two main phases: emission and expulsion.

The ejaculation process is activated by stimulating genitals (mainly penile stimulation), and also by the "erotic" brain, so it is controlled partly by touch and partly by thoughts and/or visual stimuli.

The emission phase first happens by the closure of the bladder neck, which stops the semen from going backwards into the bladder. The emission phase prepares the ejaculatory fluid (semen), which is made of:

1. Secretions from the prostate (10 per cent of the final semen volume).
2. Spermatozoa from the vas deferens (10 per cent of the volume).
3. Seminal vesicle fluid (75–80 per cent).
4. A tiny part from Cowper's and periurethral glands.

The expulsion phase follows the emission phase. The expulsion phase is the ejection of the semen through the urethra, propelled through rhythmic contractions of the pelvic floor muscles.

THE BIOLOGICAL CAUSES OF SEXUAL PROBLEMS

It is important to pay attention to sexual problems. Although sexual problems can be of a psychological nature for many people, they can also be symptoms of underlying medical problems, and they can be an indicator of undiagnosed medical issues that should be attended to. It is always a good idea to have a medical investigation when experiencing recurring sexual problems.

The most common sexual problems in AMAB people are:

- Unreliable erections.
- Rapid ejaculations.
- Delayed ejaculations.
- Loss of sexual desire.

The most common sexual problems in AFAB people are:

- Vaginismus (penetration is impossible).
- Dyspareunia (painful penetration).
- Loss of sexual desire.

Some of the medical causes are:

- Urological infections.
- Diabetes.
- Cardiovascular disease.
- High blood pressure.
- High cholesterol.
- Hormonal imbalances (including the pituitary gland malfunction).
- Neurological disorders (including multiple sclerosis (MS) and spinal cord injury).
- Nerve damage as a result of some surgical procedures.

People who drink too much alcohol or take recreational drugs can disrupt the physiological balance of the body and cause sexual problems. Many medications can also cause sexual problems, including blood pressure medications and anti-depressants. If people need surgery or if they need to be on medications for a medical issue, it is a good idea to ask their doctor about the side-effects on sexual functioning. It is often a subject doctors won't talk about and patients don't ask either. Some disabled people can face great challenges with their sexual functioning if they feel consistent body pain.

SUMMARY

It is important to know the fundamentals of the biological processes of our bodies in order to differentiate some normal functioning compared to what might be a problem. For example, the clitoris is solely for pleasure, and people with vulvas can have multiple orgasms. On the other hand, the sexual responses of people with penises require a fine balance of brain and body communication in order to have and maintain erections.

Understanding such processes helps normalise the various ways that sexual responses can happen with people of all genders, and it can give us some clues as to what might contribute to sexual problems of an organic origin. Menstruation and menopause, for example, is a process that happens to all people with an ovarian system, yet it is largely unspoken and hidden, which leaves many in the dark as to why they experience certain symptoms. It is important to note that this chapter describes the typical physiology of sex, but, as I have explained in previous chapters, the diversity of humankind means that there are wide variations. A cocktail of brain chemicals are involved in human sexual responses, arousal and orgasm, such as oxytocin (called the bonding hormone), dopamine (the reward and learning neurotransmitter), testosterone, oestrogen, and progesterone (the sex hormones), as well as others that are feel-good, healthy chemicals for the brain and body. Isn't it wonderful?

Reflective questions:

1 What have you learnt about the physiology of sex in this chapter that you didn't know before?

2 What was surprising to you about the content of this chapter?

3 What might you ask your doctor about things you haven't thought of before?

4 What clarity have you gained in your understanding of the connection between your eroticism, emotions, body in the here-and-now, your nervous system and your sex life?

FURTHER READING

What Fresh Hell Is This? Perimenopause, Menopause, Other Indignities and You, by Heather Corinna (2021).

Untrue. How surprising new science of the female libido can set us free, by Wednesday Martin (2018).

Becoming Cliterate. Why Orgasm Equality Matters – And How to Get It, by Laurie Mintz, PhD (2017).

REFERENCES

Basson, R. (2001) Human Sex-Response Cycles. *Journal of Sex & Marital Therapy*, 27(1), 33–43. doi:10.1080/00926230152035831

Gräfenberg, E. (1950). The Role of the Urethra in Female Orgasm. *The International Journal of Sexology*, 3, 145–148.

Gurney, K. (2020). *Mind The Gap. The Truth about Desire and How to Futureproof Your Sex Life*. Headline Publishing Group. London.

Kaschak, E., & Tiefer, L. (2001). *A New View of Women's Sexual Problems*. Haworth Press, Inc. Binghamton, NY.

Leeds, L., & Hargreaves, I. (2008). The Psychological Consequences of Childbirth. *Journal of Reproductive and Infant Psychology*, 26(2), 108–122. doi:10.1080/02646830701688299

Masters, W.H., & Johnson, V.E. (1966). *Human Sexual Response*. Bantam Books. Toronto; New York.

Nagoski, E. (2015). *Come As You Are. The Surprising New Science that Will Transform Your Sex Life*. Scribe Publications. London.

Singer Kaplan, H. (1974). *The New Sex Therapy. Active Treatment of Sexual Dysfunction*. Brunner/Mazel, Inc. New York.

SEXUAL BEHAVIOURS

Now that I have explained our gender diversities, our sexual orientations, our eroticism, and how our bodies respond physiologically to sexual stimuli, I'm going to discuss various sexual practices. Although some practices may be unfamiliar to you, the ones listed here are all legal, consensual, and functional. By now, you know that there is no normal in sexuality and sexual behaviours as long as it is legal and consensual. Nevertheless, you might be surprised, even shocked, by the content of this chapter. You might need to re-evaluate what you previously considered "weird" or "strange".

We cannot have thorough conversations about sexual practices without the frame of the "six principles of sexual health". These principles are helpful because they do not focus on specific behaviours, thus not instilling shame for sexual behaviours that are normative and functional. These principles aim to offer clarity on the fundamental principles of sexual health, which means that all behaviours that meet these principles may be assessed as functional. If there are any parts of sexual behaviours that fall outside one or more of these principles, it doesn't necessarily mean there is a pathology (or a disease) but it may mean that the individual needs to integrate their sexual behaviours within the principles, considering different options for reconfiguration.

THE SIX PRINCIPLES OF SEXUAL HEALTH

Braun-Harvey and Vigorito (2016) thoroughly explain the six principles of sexual health in the context of problematic sexual behaviours in their pioneering book, *Treating Out of Control Sexual Behavior,*

DOI: 10.4324/9781003276913-7

Rethinking Sex Addiction. Here, I will offer my own interpretation of those principles (adapted from my book, *Compulsive Sexual Behaviours, A Psycho-sexual Treatment Guide for Clinicians*, Neves, 2021).

1. *Consent* is the explicit permission to touch and be touched by other people. Consent is not only saying yes or no to touch, it is also being clear about what we are consenting to in a fully informed manner. We can consent to allow our body to be touched by someone else for their and/or our own pleasure, or we can touch someone's body for our own and/or their pleasure (Martin & Dalzen, 2021). Consent is only valid in the here-and-now. It means that consenting to something today shouldn't be an assumption that the same consent would be granted tomorrow. Clear and explicit consent has to be sought every single time. Consent can be withdrawn at any time. It means that as soon as there is discomfort about the activity that is happening, we can request to pause and re-establish clarity before continuing or we can choose to stop the activity altogether, which must be respected by our partner(s) immediately.

2. *Non-exploitation* is being mindful not to manipulate or coerce people by withholding some information or lying. All of us have the potential to manipulate people emotionally, psychologically, and sexually. For example, saying: "I will leave you if you don't have sex with me as often as I want" is an emotional, psychological, and sexual manipulation. Or "I don't like you wearing revealing clothes in front of my friends" may also be abusive as it is an attempt to control someone's decision to wear the clothes they wish. Some people resort to gaslighting, which means denying people's reality and making them believe they are going crazy. For example, saying: "No, I'm not cheating, it's all in your head" even if there is undeniable evidence of cheating. In fact, infidelity (also termed non-consensual non-monogamy) is an exploitation of the relationship because the withholding of the information of sexual contact with others makes it impossible for the betrayed partner to make informed choices about their own sexual health.

3. *Protection from HIV, STIs, and unwanted pregnancy* is self-explanatory, or is it? There seems to be a high rate of unwanted (or surprise) pregnancies in the UK, despite all the information

on contraception that is available. So, what is going on? People don't think enough about the consequences of sex. Sex is an adult behaviour and it requires adult thinking, which includes gathering all the information needed for informed consent but also having foresight about what might happen next. The conversation on the prevention of HIV has dramatically changed over the last few years with the introduction of PrEP (pre-exposure prophylaxis), which means that people can protect themselves against HIV without using condoms. Those who live with HIV and are adhering to their medications are likely to have an undetectable viral load that makes the transmission of HIV impossible, as the promotion of the campaign U=U explains (Undetectable = Untransmittable). This great medical progress lowered the rate of HIV infections. Yet, the battle with the virus is not over because the stigma of HIV prevails. People who are HIV positive encounter discrimination and attack on a regular basis because of their HIV status. As good as PrEP is, it doesn't prevent other STIs. Chlamydia, gonorrhoea, and syphilis are bacterial infections that can cause great damage if they are left untreated. Because they are bacteria, they can be caught quite easily and they don't always show up with symptoms for a while. That's why it is important to be tested on a regular basis. Herpes, a virus many people carry unknowingly, is not life-threatening and has either no or mild adverse effects but is not curable. Meeting this principle of sexual health requires being fully informed and taking responsibility for our own sexual health.

4. *Honesty* starts with oneself. Being curious about our own Erotic Template means that we can embrace our erotic self fully, which includes our sexual orientations and our eroticism, our gender expression and attractions, and the types of relationships we need in order to thrive. We can only be honest with others if we are honest with ourselves. Being candid is a great gift of love to our partner(s), even when it is hard to do. It takes great courage to reveal our turn-ons, but it also provides an erotic and sensual map for us and our partner(s) to help us navigate sex in a flourishing way. It also gives our sexual partner(s) an opportunity to decide whether they want to engage in such activities or not, and, together, we can decide what is similar in our Erotic Templates and how we can meet them.

5. *Shared values* are the principles that follow from honesty and encourage conversations with partner(s) to check compatibility. It is important for a good and thriving sex life that the values relevant to our sex lives are aligned with our partner(s). For example, sharing a kink together, having the same values around ethical non-monogamy, or being on the same page about important moral or religious do's and don'ts. If we are not clear about our shared values with our sexual partner(s), we could be at risk of great wounding. For example, it is important not to assume that a sexual partner has the same monogamous values if we haven't had a thorough conversation about it.

6. *Mutual pleasure* is central to the motivation of people choosing to have sex, yet it is also often dismissed and unspoken about. In most sex education, people are taught about procreation and how to avoid diseases, but not about pleasure. Our society is still quite sex-negative when it comes to discussing turn-ons and pleasure, and it seems that we are quick to judge if someone's turn-on is one that we don't understand. The principle of mutual pleasure is not about mutual orgasms. In fact, the myth that mutual orgasms are the hallmark of successful sex puts a lot of pressure on people to achieve it. In reality, people can take their time, and they can take turns to reach orgasms. Mutual pleasure means to be fully present in the here and now, and to enjoy all the pleasurable sensations that happen when we are in a sexual situation with our intimate partner(s). It might be enjoying the touch, skin-to-skin contact, the visuals, the "dirty talk", the erotic atmosphere, or the horny attitudes of our partner(s). The mutual pleasure principle is being mindful that what happens in the moment feels right for all the people involved.

Braun-Harvey and Vigorito (2016) remind us of the WHO definition of sexual health:

> Sexual Health is the possibility of having pleasurable and safe sexual experiences, free of coercion, discrimination, and violence.

As you can see, the six principles of sexual health help us understand how we conduct our sex life. We can become fully conscious and aware of our sexual behaviours. Full awareness helps us access our wisdom so that we can make the right sexual decisions for ourselves.

SEXUAL PRACTICES

Now, let's look at various sexual behaviours. Some people may initiate these behaviours on a regular basis, while others may experiment with some of them. Some of these sexual behaviours are intensely arousing for some, while they can be repulsive to others. This is by no means a definitive list of sexual behaviours because there are too many to fit in one chapter but these are some of the most common ones. I have decided to make this list alphabetical as it is the best way not to imply what is most preferable or most "normal" with the order of the list.

Abstinence is the voluntary decision to abstain from sex, even if there is sexual desire. People define their abstinence differently. Some heterosexual people understand it as not having "penis-in-vagina" sex, which means that having oral sex or anal sex is still considered abstinence. Others have a more global definition of their abstinence which includes refraining from any sexualised touch. Most people choose abstinence for religious reasons. Some people opt for abstinence as a means of contraception. Sometimes, abstinence is recommended by medical professionals for a short time after specific surgeries.

Agoraphilia is the term used for those who enjoy sex outdoors. There are some outdoor private places that can be appropriate for sex, for example a secluded back garden or a private outdoor sex club. There are outdoors public places that are known for "cruising" where people meet and have sex. It is not legal, but these places are often secluded from the general public and there is a certain amount of tolerance for these practices.

Agrexophilia refers to people whose turn-on is having sex with the possibility that they could be overheard by others. Some of those people enjoy loud sex in hotels or while spending a night at a friend's place. It can also be a turn-on for them to have sex in toilet cubicles or in a sex club.

Amaurophilia describes the turn-on of someone who enjoys having sex with someone who can't see them (using a blindfold, for example).

Anaclitism is sexual arousal from activities or objects associated with early childhood. For example, it might be the turn-on for diapers, soothers, sucking on a woman's nipple (in a role play of mother-baby). Some of those behaviours can also be considered a fetish.

Anal Intercourse is penis in rectum penetration. It is a very common practice for heterosexual people, especially women being anally receptive, but some heterosexual men love to be penetrated too. It is not a sign of being gay (see pegging). It is also a popular practice among gay and bisexual men, although not all of them practice anal sex. The definition of anal sex may extend to the insertion of objects into the anus, such as dildos, fingers, or prostate massage devices. It is important to only use objects that have been specifically designed for anal insertion. Any medical professionals working in A&E will tell you that anal sex with household objects can quickly go wrong! Anal sex can be practised with sexual partner(s) or solo. It is a practice that used to be called "sodomy" but that is now an old-fashioned word.

Anilingus is more commonly known as rimming. It is oral sex in the anal area, stimulating the anus with lips and tongue. The anal area has a lot of nerve endings, it is a sensitive area so many people find this practice extremely pleasurable. Some people who are not interested in anal intercourse may still love anilingus. It is important to take precautions such as using dental dam, as there is a risk of infection from bacteria living in the intestines and rectum.

Autoerotic Asphyxiation is the practice of self-strangulation while masturbating, with a hand or sex toy, which is thought to enhance the intensity of the orgasm due to partial asphyxiation. Doing it solo means that there is a risk of death if an accident happens during the practice.

Autofellatio is licking and sucking one's own penis. It is perhaps the wish of many people, yet only a few are able to do this because it takes a lot of muscle flexibility to contort the body in such a way to make it possible.

Barebacking is the sexual practice of having intercourse without condoms. Although people of all sexual orientations practise this sexual behaviour, the term bareback is usually used within the context of gay men's sexual behaviours. Among gay men and men who have sex with men (MSM), there is a strong bareback sub-culture, partly to reclaim sexual rights of pleasure, pushing back against the homophobic ostracisation and recapturing autonomy after the prohibition of barebacking during the AIDS epidemic. Many people report an enhanced sense of connection and pleasure with bareback sex that cannot be replicated with condom sex. Luckily, the advance of PrEP made this practice safer, although it doesn't eliminate the risks of contracting other sexually transmitted infections. There is still much taboo, stigma, and judgement about bareback behaviours.

Body Rubbing is also known as dry humping or frottage. This is when sexual partners rub their bodies together, especially around the genital areas, fully clothed. Some people love this practice as it can be considered safe sex, and it can be pleasurable enough to the extent of producing an orgasm. This practice needs to be done privately between consenting adults, if it is done in public, for example on a crowded public transport with strangers who have not consented to it, it is a sexual offence.

BDSM stands for bondage, discipline, submission, and sadomasochism. It is a group of sexual practices that is now well-known yet still widely misunderstood. There is a huge range of different sexual practices that are under the umbrella of BDSM, but broadly it involves power play, and for some, pain, such as spanking or flogging. Some sexual partner(s) identify as "bottom" or "sub": they enjoy being in the submissive role, sometimes restrained, sometimes consensually punished. Some sexual partner(s) take the role of the "top" or "Dom": those who enjoy dominating and taking control of the sexual activities (the capital "D" and lower case "s" are part of the code of "Dom/sub" play). Some people identify as a "switch", which means they can move between being in the submissive role and the Dominant role. The BDSM communities are very strong with their mindset of practice:

(1) Safe: although there may be some spanking, body restraint, and other hard-hitting practices, they need to remain safe in terms of bodily integrity and not require significant medical care afterwards. BDSMers use a safe word that indicates when the practice becomes too intense and needs to stop immediately.

(2) Sane: not being under the influence of substances that can make consent impossible and to remain fully conscious of what is going on so that they can stay within full control of the practice.

(3) Consensual: every single element of the practice is discussed beforehand, planned, and needs to be fully consented to at all times. There is a strong understanding that consent can be withdrawn at any time and the practice has to stop immediately.

If someone is interested in BDSM, I strongly suggest that they take their time, meet the BDSM communities, and talk to them to learn from them before launching into it. Some elements of BDSM have landed on the mainstream sexual "menu" of people, for example, handcuffs, blindfolds, or light spanking. Many people practice a very mild version of power play that may be considered kinky yet people may still identify as "vanilla".

For some people, BDSM is a sexual leisure activity (they can do it sometimes but not all the time), while for some others, it is an erotic orientation (they need to practise it most of the time in order to feel sexually satisfied). Despite the popular misinformation, there is no link between BDSM and childhood trauma.

Coitus means penis-in-vagina intercourse, also known as copulation, vaginal intercourse, or simply sexual intercourse. The practice usually describes the movement of the penis back and forth inside the vagina until ejaculation happens. Traditionally, coitus was known as primarily a reproductive practice, which required ejaculation, so it was thought that the orgasm of people with penises was needed, but there was very little consideration for the orgasm of people with vaginas. As I explained in Chapter 5, many people with vaginas do not experience orgasms with penetration.

Coitus a mammilla is a practice when a person stimulates their penis between a person's breasts, often to the point of ejaculation. This is a practice popular with heterosexual people and is especially exciting for people with penises who have a fetish of people with big breasts (usually cisgender women's breasts).

Coprophilia is also known as "scat play" or "scatology". It is a sexual practice that involves human faeces. Although the thought of faeces provokes reactions of disgust for many people, it can produce sexual arousal and pleasure for some. People who are interested in coprophilia particularly enjoy the smell or the texture of faeces. Some are turned on by the cornerstone of eroticism of "violating prohibition". Coprophilia can be practised in different ways. Some people are turned on by watching someone else defecate. These people often describe a sense of deep connection at sharing something so intimate and private. Others prefer touching faeces, from smearing their own faeces or somebody else's on their bodies or being defecated on. For some, it is linked with being a "sub" (being used as a toilet). Some consider anilingus to be coprophilia when the turn-on involves rimming an unclean anus.

Cuckolding is the kink of being turned on by a partner having sex with someone else, consensually. It is often related to the kink of Domination, submission, and humiliation. The person being cuckolded will often enjoy the scenario of being humiliated by their partner's choice of a separate sexual partner for being better in bed than them. The humiliation usually relates to their penis being too small and the sexual partner of choice being well-endowed, often called "a bull". It is a popular kink among heterosexual and LGBTQ+ people.

Cunnilingus is the practice of stimulating the vulva with oral sex (lips and tongue). The labia and the clitoris are licked and sucked, but it is the focus on the clitoris that produces the most pleasure for women and people with vulvas. This is usually practised as a means to prepare the body for penis-in-vagina penetration among heterosexual people, however, it can be a practice done by itself until orgasm is reached. There is a myth that sex automatically means penetration and cunnilingus is often perceived as the "warm-up" or foreplay, but in fact, it can be considered as sex in and of itself. Cunnilingus is indeed its own sex practice among lesbians, but not all lesbians practise it.

Cybersex is defined by accessing sexual arousal and pleasure through online practices, which includes masturbating with someone else on webcam, or watching/being watched masturbating. It may include the use of chat rooms, specialist apps, sexual computer games, and the creation of an avatar having sex with other avatars in a virtual world. People who love feeling sexual pleasure by masturbating while watching pornography may also identify it as cybersex. It can be practised by people in monogamous and committed relationships who live in different places, as well as practised among casual sexual partners or strangers (it was a very popular practice during the COVID-19 pandemic). Some people enjoy these practices very much and can do it sometimes. Others primarily enjoy cybersex in order to feel fully sexually satisfied, they may self-identify as Digisexual (see Chapter 3).

Dogging is a term describing people enjoying couples (or other people) having sex in their car in a car park. This is an overlap with exhibitionism and voyeurism. Although it is technically illegal as it is considered public sex, there are car parks known for these activities and it is usually done at night when there are fewer people around, so it is a practice that is tolerated.

Erotic Massage is the sensual practice of a full body massage done by one or more people who are naked or partially naked, massaging the erogenous parts of the body and focusing on genitals for sexual pleasure until reaching an orgasm. Most massages involve the hands, but some people massage with their full body, mouth (oral sex included), and some progress the massage into intercourse (vaginal or anal). Some erotic massage includes fingers inserted in the anus for a prostate massage, which is often intensely pleasurable. The massage of the vulva, clitoral stimulation, and finger insertion in the vagina may also produce intense pleasure and orgasm (it is commonly called "Yoni massage"). These erotic massages are often practised by people who have been trained in tantric massage.

Exhibitionism is the sexual arousal of being watched, either undressing, naked, in intimate and private spaces, having sex with other people, or masturbating in front of others. Sometimes exhibitionism is enjoyed in a nudist public place, but not all people enjoying nudist spaces are turned on by exhibitionism. Some exhibitionists are turned on by *autagonistophilia*, feeling aroused by being on stage or performing for someone, like someone filming them, for example. If exhibitionism is practised among consenting adults, it can be a highly pleasurable practice. Exhibitionism in a common public space (not a nudist area) and with non-consenting adults or with children is a criminal offence.

Feederism is the fetish of erotic eating. Feeders are turned on by feeding others and feedees are sexually aroused by being fed by other people. Both the feeder and feedee's fetish may be linked to being sexually aroused by weight gaining and/or power play, when the feeder plays a Dominant role and the feedee a submissive one.

Fellatio is oral sex stimulating a penis, by licking or sucking with the lips, mouth, and tongue. It may include licking and sucking the scrotum too (commonly called *tea-bagging*). Sometimes, this practice is used as foreplay to prepare the penis for penetration, but it can also be a sexual practice in and of itself, leading to orgasm. The use of the semen produced at the point of ejaculation may be an integral part of the pleasure of fellatio; some people love swallowing the semen while others prefer to receive it on their face or on a part of their body (breast, chest, buttock, genitals, feet, etc.). For gay and bisexual men who do not like anal sex, fellatio can be their main sexual practice. They often identify as "sides", a term coined by Dr Joe Kort.

Felching describes a practice of licking semen out of the vagina or anus after intercourse that finished with ejaculation inside it.

Fetishism may be an erotic orientation (see Chapter 4). It describes sexual arousal in response to a specific object (shoes, food, silk, rubber, leather, etc.), a body part that is non-genital (breasts, feet, legs, armpits, hair, ears, etc.), or a practice (cross-dressing, role play, etc.). Many people can integrate their fetish into their erotic and sexual life very well, which is intensely pleasure enhancing. Some fetishes may be considered a "disorder" if it causes distress in people's lives, although this is controversial and hotly debated.

Findom, meaning financial Domination, refers to the kink of Dominant people demanding money from submissive people. Both Dominant and submissive people experience an erotic thrill around money. It is also linked to the kink of humiliation as the submissive will perceive their Dominant partner as better than them. Findom can be practised safely when the Dominant and submissive people fully agree on the boundaries of the play and it does not cause significant financial distress. In other words, the submissive person needs to be able to assess what they can comfortably afford before agreeing on the play. There is a high risk of financial exploitation with this practice when the findom is not genuine and the practice is a disguise for financial abuse.

Fisting is the practice of inserting a hand into the vagina or rectum of a sexual partner(s). Usually, the fist is moved in and out or with rhythmic movements inside it. This practice needs much care and a lot of preparation with gradual stretching of the vagina or anus. It is considered a form of kink, and it is most widely practised within the communities of kinky gay men. Some report this practice to be both pleasure and connection enhancing as they feel the most emotionally connected to their partner(s) through the practice.

Foot fetish is also called *podophilia*, and it is a very common fetish among people of all sexual orientations and gender identities. The practice includes masturbating while watching someone's feet (consensually), giving or receiving foot massages, rubbing parts of the body on the feet, kissing the feet, or licking toes. It may also include wearing specific footwear (stilettos, sandals, trainers, boots, for example), or wearing socks (white, clean, dirty or smelly, for example).

Foreplay describes the behaviours that have the purpose of preparation for penetrative sex. Most people misunderstand what foreplay is, thinking it is oral sex or manual stimulation, and believing that "real" sex is penetrative sex. In fact, oral sex and manual stimulation are forms of legitimate, real, sex by themselves and having sex doesn't need to include penetration at all. People launch into sexual practices like oral sex and manual stimulation thinking it is foreplay but they are not actually doing the proper preparation for penetrative sex (which is the real foreplay). Proper foreplay (which means before play) includes talking about sex and sharing erotic ideas, having a thorough conversation of consent about what is going to happen sexually, deciding how to engage in mutual pleasure, getting the necessary practical things ready like the unwrapped condom, lube, towels or whatever people want and need for a good experience such as candles, music, specific bedding, etc. Foreplay is preparing the body too, for example making sure not to have too full a stomach when the body goes into digestion, making sure the level of energy is adequate (not when people are too tired), and paying attention to hygiene. After that, the next stage of foreplay can be kissing, undressing each other, and moving towards sex. Although all of these may sound "unsexy", they are essential foreplay ingredients. "Unsexy" doesn't mean no fun. With the cornerstone of eroticism of "anticipation", it is possible to make the foreplay a lot of fun! In fact, it might be more helpful to change the term "fore-play" to "main-play" or "core-play" as it's this part of sex that generates the most pleasure and orgasm for some people.

Furries are people who enjoy wearing animal costumes, usually colourful and cartoon character-like animals rather than realistic animals while having sex. Some who identify as furries are more sensually or psychologically turned on rather than sexually turned on by the costumes. They enjoy being around others or parading with the costumes rather than having sex. On the other hand, some love having sex in costumes, in one-to-one and group sex settings. Some are heavily involved in the subculture of furries' fan groups.

Group sex is a sexual activity that involves more than two partners at the same time. It is often known as an orgy. There are many different ways to practise group sex. Some who are in relationships have sex with others in relationships, some prefer to have sex with multiple people who are strangers. Some go to specific places that cater for group sex, for example, a sex club, while others prefer to engage in group sex in private parties organised in someone's home. Group sex can be composed of different sexual orientations and genders. In mixed-sex group sex, some may identify as heterosexual, bisexual, or gay. It may be in those settings that some will allow themselves to experience sexual and intimate touch from people who do not strictly fit with the definition of their sexual orientation, for example, a man who identifies as heterosexual having erotic touch with another man in the context of group sex involving women too (as I have discussed in Chapter 3, sexuality can be fluid). Some group sex may have specific themes, for example BDSM themes, fetish themes (leather dress-code, or nudist, for example), or a specific purpose such as a "gang bang", which is one person being vaginally or anally receptive to multiple penetrating partners, in a queue, one at a time. Some group sex can involve being in a "sandwich" or "spit-roast", which means being penetrated anally or vaginally while giving oral sex to someone else. Once again, all of these practices have to be fully consensual between adults.

Holiday/hotel sex is on this list because it is widely reported that many people feel highly sexual when they are in a new and unfamiliar place (*hodophilia*). This turn-on usually presents itself when people go on holiday or when they are in a new hotel room. This is why many couples often say that they have their best sexual moments while on holiday. It is also why many infidelities happen when one is on a business trip, in a hotel.

Hotwifing is a term used by people sharing their very attractive wife with others for sexual pleasure. It is usually done within heterosexual relationships. Hotwifing is a different kink from cuckolding. While cuckolding is centred around Domination, submission, and humiliation, hotwifing, on the other hand, is about feeling proud to have a "hot wife", celebrating her beauty and eroticism, and sharing her.

Masturbation is the practice of stimulating one's genitals with a hand, fingers, or masturbation toys. It is a non-penetrative practice (unless the person has a penis and is using a sex toy such as a fleshlight), often done solo, but can be done with a partner present. Some people practice mutual masturbation, which is stimulating each other's genitals. Or one person can masturbate another for their pleasure. Solo masturbation is often done with the aid of pornography (especially for men), but women can access arousing pornography that is made by women for women, which is often more attractive to them than the mainstream pornography catering for men. Some don't need pornography as they can enjoy masturbation using their own erotic fantasies. Some practise mindful masturbation which is the focus on the body sensations of masturbation. The practice of masturbation can be stigmatised and considered "wrong" (as is the use of pornography, see Chapter 7). Some people feel shame for masturbating, especially if they have accessed misinformation about the "benefits" of quitting masturbation. This is usually misinformation (and pseudo-science) directed at men, promoting that, somehow, "semen retention" elevates their potency of masculinity, and so on. This is inaccurate. There are literally no health benefits of abstaining from masturbation. Equally, choosing not to masturbate for one reason or another, won't harm people. However, masturbation is a great resource for stress-relief, soothing, and emotional regulation. Masturbation also keeps the genital area healthy by promoting blood flow, reducing atrophy and maintaining erectile tissue in penises and vulvas. On the other hand, feeling guilty about masturbation can lead to depression (Chakrabarti et al., 2002).

Mummification is part of the BDSM practice of bondage when one's entire body is wrapped, making the person unable to move. There is sometimes an agreement that the genitals, nipples, or anus are left exposed for sexual play while in mummification. Just as with all other BDSM practices, thorough consensual conversations are required, including the use of a safe word, before engaging in this kind of activity.

Pegging is a heterosexual practice when a woman (usually cisgender) anally penetrates a man (usually cisgender) with fingers, sex toys, or using a strap-on. This is a taboo practice mostly because heterosexual men are worried that their love for being anally penetrated means that they are gay. Of course, this sexual practice has nothing to do with being gay, and a lot to do with enjoying prostate stimulation.

Phone sex is having sexually explicit conversations with other people on the phone. It is usually accompanied by masturbation to the point of reaching an orgasm. Some phone sex includes sexual stories or some arousing conversations framed as sexual confessions. Some phone sex may involve a sub/Dom role play with consensual sexual commands or suggestions. Phone sex can be practised by people in monogamous and committed relationships who live in different places, as well as practised among casual sexual partners or strangers. Phone sex is somewhat less popular now because of the technological advances that made cybersex more accessible. Yet, some people still find phone sex a major turn-on.

Pup play is a kinky practice predominantly done by gay men in the leather fetish communities. A pup is a person who enjoys dressing up as a dog, but unlike furries, they do not have fur, they wear a leather outfit, with a mask resembling a dog's face and the tail is a special butt plug. Pups aren't single people, they typically have an "owner" or "master" who looks after them, plays with them, and loves them. This kinky practice usually involves sexual behaviours such as oral and anal sex, but not always.

Role play is the sexual play of acting out a fantasy, a story or being a character that is out of everyday life. It can be a great way to spice up people's sex lives, especially those in long-term relationships. Role play varies greatly from mild to wild depending on people's erotic minds. For some, it may be pretending to be a doctor and a patient, or boss and employee. Or it may be meeting a romantic partner, pretending they're a stranger in a bar. Or it could be kinkier, including some BDSM practices. Some people have specific role plays depending on their specific turn-on. For example, someone with *harpaxophilia* (the turn-on from being robbed) may choose to have specific robbery fantasies or role plays to enhance their sex life, although it would obviously be an unwelcome experience if it happened in real life. Some people enjoy doing role plays on a frequent basis to have a fulfilling sex life, while others choose to practise it only occasionally.

Safe Sex refers to having sex in a way that it prevents the contraction of STIs. The term "safe sex" is quite misleading because in reality there are very few sexual practices that are safe sex, for example, masturbation, and consensual frottage. Most other sexual practices have an element of risk, but calculated risk (just as driving a car is never truly safe but within calculated risks). Therefore, the better term is "safer sex". Most people are diligent enough to look after their sexual health by wearing a condom for vaginal or anal intercourse, but they do not enjoy oral sex with a condom. Unprotected oral sex carries the risk of contraction of chlamydia, gonorrhoea, syphilis, and herpes. There is also a risk of contracting HIV through oral sex if a person has bleeding gums, a cut, or ulcer in their mouth – it is a low risk but still a risk. Luckily, in Western countries, STIs are well-treated (people living with HIV on the appropriate medications can have good and healthy lives). To maintain sexual pleasure, some people need to consider their sexual health carefully by making the right calculated risk to achieve their best safer sex practices.

Shower, in the sexual context, involves pouring some liquid over a partner for sexual arousal. The most popular liquid is milk but it can be other things too, like custard. You will see at the end of this list, in the watersports section, that there is a specific shower called the "Golden Shower" which involves urine.

Sixty-nine is the practice of mutual oral sex with a partner at the same time. It is a common practice popular with people of all sexual orientations and gender identities.

Swinging means exchanging sexual partners between couples for extra sexual fun. Some couples prefer to play together with other couples, which can also be described as group sex. Some people call swinging the practice of inviting a third person and having sex with them, which is also called a threesome. Swinging tends to be a term mostly used by heterosexual people (people in the LGBTQ+ communities tend to use the terms "threesome", "friends with benefits", or "group sex").

Vanilla refers to sex that is not kinky or within the BDSM range. It is important to note that the term does not mean "normal", nor does it imply the qualities of loving, caring, or romantic because many kinky sex and BDSM practices are indeed normal, loving, caring, and romantic. Vanilla also does not mean "boring". It is inaccurate to think that kinky sex is exciting and colourful and by contrast vanilla is bland and boring. Vanilla and kink are not opposites, they are just different. Vanilla is, in fact, an exotic and delicate flavour that is versatile and can be adapted for many different tastes. If you have enough imagination, you won't run out of ways to have vanilla sex.

Voyeurism is the partner of exhibitionism. It is the practice of gaining sexual pleasure from watching others when they are naked or engaged in sexual activity. Usually, someone whose turn-on is exhibitionism would need partners who are into voyeurism for both practices to be fully consensual. People who enjoy voyeurism are usually people who are visually stimulated, with a strong component of visual as their Erotic Booster. Some prefer to practise voyeurism in full view of the exhibitionist, sometimes masturbating, sometimes not. Some prefer to be hidden away from the exhibitionist's view, as long as the exhibitionist has consented to be watched/spied on. The practice of a person consensually watching a couple have sex is also called *candaulism*. Voyeurism is illegal if someone is watching someone else without consent.

Watersports also called *urophilia* (arousal from urine) or "golden shower". It refers to urinating on a partner, urinating on oneself, or watching someone else urinate. Some people find this practice extremely arousing.

MOTIVATION FOR SEX

The range of human sexual behaviours is very wide, based on our specific turn-ons, desire, arousal, how our body works, our sense of self-esteem, and connection. But do we know where our motivation for our sexual behaviours comes from in the first place? It turns out that there are 237 reasons that lead human beings to have sex, according to research by Meston and Buss (2007). Some of the most common physical reasons are "stress reduction, pleasure, physical desirability and experience seeking". The common goal-attainment reasons are "resources, social status, revenge and utilitarian" (in this context, utilitarian means practical reasons such as relieving a period pain). The common emotional reasons are "love, commitment, and expression". And the insecurity factors are "self-esteem boost, duty/pressure, and mate guarding".

While having sexual desire is innate in most of us, having sex isn't. It is mostly learnt and it requires understanding our erotic mind and our body very well. It also involves learning skills and understanding our motivations. In order to achieve a fulfilling sex life, we must have good sex education, know about our boundaries within the six principles of sexual health, and also be kinder to each other by understanding that we are all different. What matters is that we express clearly to our potential sexual partner(s) what we need and want in order to engage in sexual behaviours in a way that is enhancing, fulfilling, and leaves us feeling at peace about it. Indeed, sexual satisfaction doesn't just happen. It requires time, patience, communication, and self-awareness.

The reason for having sex is not one answer-fits-all. I would like to suggest being cautious when we hear some statements of certainty about the judgement of other people's sexual behaviours. People's sex lives are not easily defined by generalisations. For example, some of the blanket statements that we might hear and believe are:

- People who are sex workers are damaged people.
- People who like scat are in arrested development.
- Watching too much porn will lead to sexual offending.
- Choosing an open relationship is avoiding problems in a monogamous relationship.

Such sweeping statements can do more harm than good. It is important to stay curious with our erotic mind, the answers live with us, in our own erotic wisdom, not from someone else who doesn't live in our mind and body.

SEXUAL SATISFACTION

When people embrace their gender identities, sexual orientations, their eroticism (the content of their erotic mind, what turns them on/off), and understand the physiology of sex, they are more likely to experience sexual satisfaction. The more people know themselves, the easier it is to navigate the erotic space. Because of the vast diversity of human beings, the ingredients to sexual satisfaction will be different from one person to another. However, there are also some universal components to sexual satisfaction:

- Physical pleasure: experiencing pleasure in the sexual experience, as well as orgasm.
- A desire for erotic connection, or emotional intimacy, even if it is with a one-off sexual encounter.
- The quality of the relationship enhancing the sexual experience. There is more sexual satisfaction if the relationship(s) is warm, loving, caring, and respectful. It is particularly relevant in an established relationship, but it can apply to a one-off sexual encounter when the short-term connection is strong (some people call it the "sexual chemistry").

As well as the components to sexual satisfaction that are universal, there are some that are specific to trans people and nonbinary people (Lindley et al., 2021; Goldbach et al., 2022):

- Being with a partner (or several partners) that understands the experiences of being a trans and nonbinary person, affirming and respecting boundaries.
- Affirmation of gender identity from partner(s) during sex. Even small affirmations will do.
- Being comfortable in their bodies, finding sexual positions and perhaps clothing that can minimise gender dysphoria.

PROBLEMATIC SEXUAL BEHAVIOURS

I would like to note briefly here that although many sexual behaviours are normative, even those who appear unusual or strange, we need to recognise that some people feel distressed by some of their sexual behaviours. They might express their distress by calling themselves "weird", "broken", being "out of control", or even a "sex addict". They would certainly say their behaviours and preferences are problematic for them.

The term "problematic" needs to be unpacked as we can often fear people mean illegal behaviours when they use this word. Many of the sexual behaviours that people describe as problematic are not illegal and are done between consenting adults. The problematic behaviours that are illegal and non-consensual will be explored in Chapter 9. Here, I would like to discuss the behaviours that people describe as problematic but are legal.

Most people will describe their problematic behaviours as having too much sex, watching too much pornography, masturbating too much, having ongoing unresolved sexual problems with their partner(s), cheating on their partner(s) on a regular basis, or doing things that they simply don't feel right about. Exploring the source of the distress is important because the problem often lies in what Braun-Harvey and Vigorito (2016) identify as "erotic conflicts", which means that people are stuck in "competing needs" between satisfying their erotic turn-ons, or their wants and desires, and their commitment with their partner(s), the societal or religious inhibitions, and what they "should" do. People can be helped with assessing their behaviours by checking if they meet the six principles of sexual health.

Although "sex addiction" is a popular term to describe repetitive and unwanted sexual behaviours, it is not the clinical term that is endorsed by APA (DSM-5) nor by WHO (ICD-11). In fact, the term "sex addiction" is quite unhelpful because it perpetuates a narrative of disease, it has its roots in heteronormativity and sex–negative beliefs about sexual behaviours, and it is shaming. Chasioti and Binnie (2021) found that using the addiction language of "sobriety" and "relapse" can maintain people's distress. The only diagnostic criteria that clinical sexologists have to assess compulsive sexual behaviours are classified under impulse control, not addiction. This is an important distinction because knowing what this problem is – and is not – can help people find the right treatments. I don't recommend an addiction treatment for a problem that is not an addiction. Some "sex addiction" therapies and 12-step programmes can be at high risk of crossing into "conversion therapy" because of their lack of robust knowledge in contemporary sexology, mistaking normative sexual behaviours for a pathology. For example, people with a kink in BDSM, those enjoying multiple partnered sex, those preferring to watch pornography over human-contact sex are all vulnerable to being labelled "unhealthy" and a "sex addict" (Neves, 2021).

Although non-consensual non-monogamy (cheating) is not recommended because it is unethical for the relationship and partner(s), instead of shaming them and attempting to turn them into a "good monogamous romantic partner", we can help people better by supporting them to unpack the functions of their behaviours, what they get out of them, what purpose the behaviours have in their lives, what are their motivations, what personal stories underpin cheating behaviours, and what is the content of their erotic mind (Perel, 2017).

SUMMARY

The popular saying goes: "different strokes for different folks". Indeed, this chapter (or perhaps this entire book) is all about that. We like to be stroked (touched) in a particular way by particular people in particular settings and arrangements. There simply cannot be a guide of what is right or wrong. We cannot make an assumption or a judgement on somebody else's sexual behaviours just because theirs are different from ours. All that we have is the boundary of the law, what is legal and what is not. The hard boundary comes with the assessment of harm to ourselves or others, and the presence or absence of full consent. There are some sexual behaviours that are central to our sex life, some that are top favourites that we want to do most of the time when we have sex, and there are some sexual behaviours that may be more peripheral, an addition to our sex life, once in a while, for extra fun. There are sexual behaviours we never tried before but that we might have an interest in exploring, just to experiment, and there are some that are a definite no-go area, with zero interest. There are some sexual behaviours that are legal but some of us find problematic, let's be curious and try to understand those problems. "Different strokes for different folks" is the meaning of tolerance and acceptance.

Reflective questions:

1 What has surprised you about this chapter?

2 What are the sexual behaviours you read about that made you feel uncomfortable or repulsed? Do you know why?

3 What are the sexual behaviours you read about that made you feel warm or awakened your erotic mind? Do you know why?

4 How do you understand the link between your eroticism (your Erotic Template) and your sexual behaviours? Do they match? Or is there some mismatch?

5 What clarity have you gained between your sexual fantasies that you want to act upon in your sex life and those you want to keep as fantasies after reading this chapter?

6 How might you check your own judgement and automatic thoughts or assumptions when you hear of sexual behaviours that you don't understand or have never heard of before?

7 What do you consider to be problematic sexual behaviours that are legal?

FURTHER READING

Anal Pleasure and Health. 4th Revisited Edition, by Jack Morin, PhD (2010).

Decoding Your Kink. Guide to Explore Share and Enjoy Your Wildest Sexual Desires, by Galen Fous MTP (2015).

Sex Ed. A Guide for Adults, by Ruby Rare (2020).

REFERENCES

Braun-Harvey D., & Vigorito, M.A. (2016). *Treating Out of Control Sexual Behavior. Rethinking Sex Addiction.* Springer Publishing Company, LLC. New York.

Chakrabarti, N., Chopra, V.K., & Sinha, V.K. (2002). Masturbatory Guilt Leading to Severe Depression and Erectile Dysfunction. *Journal of Sex & Marital Therapy*, 28(4), 285–287. doi:10.1080/00926230290001402

Chasioti, D., & Binnie, J. (2021). Exploring the Etiological Pathways of Problematic Pornography Use in NoFap/PornFree Rebooting Communities: A Critical Narrative Analysis of Internet Forum Data. *Archives of Sexual Behavior*, 50, 2227–2243. doi:10.1007/s10508-021-01930-z

Goldbach, C., Lindley, L., Anzani, A., & Galupo, M.P. (2022) Resisting Trans Medicalization: Body Satisfaction and Social Contextual Factors as Predictors of Sexual Experiences among Trans Feminine and Nonbinary Individuals. *The Journal of Sex Research*. doi:10.1080/00224499.2021.2004384

Lindley, L., Anzani, A., Prunas, A., & Galupo, M.P. (2021). Sexual Satisfaction in Trans Masculine and Nonbinary Individuals: A Qualitative Investigation. *The Journal of Sex Research*, 58(2), 222–234. doi:10.1080/00224499.2020. 1799317

Martin, B., & Dalzen, R. (2021). *The Art of Receiving and Giving. The Wheel of Consent*. Luminare Press. Eugene, OR.

Meston, C.M., & Buss, D.M. (2007). Why Humans Have Sex. *Archives of Sexual Behavior*, 36, 477–507. doi:10.1007/s10508-007-9175-2

Neves, S. (2021). *Compulsive Sexual Behaviours. A Psycho-Sexual Treatment Guide for Clinicians*. Routledge. Abingdon, Oxon.

Perel, E. (2017). *The State of Affairs. Rethinking Infidelity*. Yellow Kite. London.

PORNOGRAPHY

Pornography is an area that is hotly debated in public discourse, provoking much emotive reaction and even arguments. This is partly because there is much confusion about pornography as it is a topic that intersects with sexology, politics, morality, religion, and legal matters. The emotive nature of the conversations about pornography, in addition to the shame and stigma because it is associated with sex and masturbation, creates a lot of confounding "noise", perpetuating what is commonly called "the porn panic". In this chapter, I'm going to bring some clarity to reduce the conflation of all these intersections with some evidence-based and balanced information.

OPINIONS OR FACTS

Reading this chapter may be challenging for some readers because it is possible that it will contradict some strong beliefs about pornography. Rothschild (2021) eloquently writes:

> I have always been of the belief that differing points of view are necessary for the growth and development of any field of study.
>
> (p. xvii)

She goes on to assert:

> The thing about knowledge is that it changes all the time – that is how it evolves ... science consists of approximation that we use until better ones come along ... It is the very normal process

DOI: 10.4324/9781003276913-8

of knowledge and professional development. Where it can be a problem is when approximations are taken to be certainty.

(pp. xviii–xix)

It is with this in mind that I wrote this entire book, but it is most particularly pertinent to remind ourselves of this when approaching the conversation about pornography. Much of the porn panic is presented as fact, when it is only speculation and, sadly, much of it is also motivated by morality (Barnett, 2016). Even though in our private lives we might hate porn or we might have unpleasant feelings about it, it is not right to impose those views on the rest of the population by perpetuating a panic because it can be shaming for those who like watching pornography without it causing any problems in their lives or other people's lives. Whatever we feel personally about pornography, keeping the humility to give up being certain about it allows more constructive and intelligent debates.

Professor Andrew Przybylski (2021) illustrates this point very well in the article he wrote for the magazine *Science Focus* in the context of responding to a common assumption that social media is bad for young people:

It's not that social media is good or bad for people. It's that the science of social media and mental health is broken. We need to do research, but we shouldn't be approaching it from the perspective that the world is ending. We need to be curious and open to the possibility of its effects, positive and negative. For instance, in recent years, we've learnt, pretty conclusively, that violent video games don't cause real-world aggression. There's nearly a perfect negative correlation between youth crime and the sale of violent video games globally. And when we revisit some of the studies from the early 2000s that were heralded as reasons for regulation, none of their findings are replicated.

If we look at our history of fear, we tend to be afraid of the advance of technology. Romantic fiction book publications were once considered corrupting of the mind of young women. The invention of the telephone brought fear that it would be easier for people to cheat and break marriages. The same goes for online pornography. We should be able to discuss the pros and cons without a "doomsday" mindset.

WHAT IS PORNOGRAPHY?

In our modern times, we automatically associate pornography with explicit hardcore films of people having sex that are easily available online. However, the actual definition of pornography is not so straightforward. It means different things to different people; it is subjective and it depends on people's cultural context as well as their expectations of it. As I discussed in Chapter 1, explicit sexual images and sculptures have existed since the beginning of humankind. Of course, what we deem as pornographic has changed since because of technology. One of the frightening theories about online pornography is its easy access that can encourage problematic use to a level previously unknown. This is commonly called "AAA" (anonymous, affordable, accessible). Indeed, it is anonymous because anybody can access online pornography without stepping out of their home. Before online pornography, people had to go to a shop to buy their porn magazines, risking being seen. It is affordable because it is virtually free. And it is accessible because all we need is a smartphone. Some people think that our brains are not designed to sustain such stimulation and frequent use and can cause psychological harm. When we think of pornography through this lens, it can feel scary. One of the anxiety-inducing beliefs is that porn can easily invade the home and family space, re-wiring the brains of our loved ones.

McKee et al. (2020) propose that defining pornography is complex because it encompasses:

> two incompatible definitions of pornography – one which says that pornographicness is a quality of texts, one saying it is produced by cultural context.

This means that pornography is understood as being a media that has the primary use of sexual arousal, but that it may be different depending on the cultural context and therefore definitions will vary from culture to culture. People are aroused by some types of pornography and not others. In Western countries, sexual material would need to be quite hardcore and explicit to be considered pornographic, while in some other countries, where nakedness is prohibited, the show of a bare ankle may be considered pornographic. In summary, pornography is highly subjective.

PROBLEMATIC USE OF PORNOGRAPHY

When we think of the problems with pornography, we automatically think of "porn addiction". The belief that porn is addictive doesn't only exist with members of the public. Some clinicians, psychotherapists, and sex therapists have that belief too, many offering treatments for it. The research in pornography has grown exponentially in the last few years, and the current scientific conclusion is that there is insufficient evidence to prove or endorse the pathology of "porn addiction" (Ley, 2016; Kohut et al. 2017; Binnie and Reavy, 2020; Charig et al., 2020). The rule of thumb is to beware of the therapists who claim the existence of "porn addiction" with certainty, citing research that sounds good but is sprinkled with pseudo-science and, often, a hidden moral agenda. You may notice that those same therapists make a profit selling "recovery" programmes for "porn addiction". The conceptualisation of "porn addiction" (as well as "sex addiction" and "love addiction" for that matter) is not clinically endorsed by the DSM-5 (APA, 2013), nor the World Health Organization's ICD-11 (International Classification of Diseases, 2019). Grubbs et al. (2020a) conducted a major independent review of the research published in "sex addiction" over the last 25 years and found:

> much of this work is characterized by simplistic methodological designs, a lack of theoretical integration, and an absence of quality measurement

Indeed, many studies on porn do not take into consideration the role of masturbation, which is odd given that most people watch pornography while masturbating. Perry (2020) suggests that when masturbation is included in the assessment of pornography use, there is a positive association between pornography use and relational happiness. Another study by Grubbs et al. (2020b) discusses the phenomenon of moral incongruence and found that people with higher religiosity are more likely to think that they have "porn addiction" even if their use is relatively moderate.

The body of research in pornography has not only found an absence of pathology, but it has also found that perpetuating the beliefs of "porn addiction" can actually cause harm. One of those studies, also mentioned in the previous chapter, suggests that a mindset of addiction and "relapse" can maintain people's distress about their pornography use, rather than being helpful (Chasioti and Binnie, 2021). Moreover, Chakrabarti et al. (2002) find that feeling guilty about masturbation can lead to depression and erection problems.

The ethos of clinical sexology and psychotherapy is to be diligent with what we promote, which needs to be strongly evidence-based to protect the public from inappropriate treatments, and to uphold our main ethical consideration: first, do no harm. Given the recent research in the potential harm of an addiction-oriented framework, professionals need to seriously reconsider their clinical position on this matter (Neves, 2021).

When we try to impose our dislike of porn on the public, we create FEAR. I saw this acronym on Instagram, from an anonymous source:

F – False
E – Evidence
A – Appearing
R – Real

I really like this because it beautifully sums up the current status quo about the current "porn panic". If we stay with fear, we can't think about it critically.

There is no universal agreement among clinicians on how to define "problematic use of porn". If we use the ICD-11 (WHO) criteria for compulsive sexual behaviours, problematic use of porn may be defined as using it to the extent that other areas of life are neglected; personal care, social engagement, life's other obligations, and so on, and cause significant distress, but the distress cannot be because of external judgements. As you can see, problematic porn use is not about frequency, but it is about an assessment of how integrated, or not, the behaviour is in a person's life. This is, of course, in the context of the use of legal porn. Accessing illegal material, or exposing children to porn, are offences punishable by law. They are different problems, which I will explain in Chapter 9.

THE PROS AND CONS OF PORNOGRAPHY

One of the most fundamental principles of sexology is to have balanced thinking. I enjoy hanging out in the unknown and the unpredictability of the grey areas because it is where the most exciting questioning and reflection emerge, rather than living in the absolute certainty of binary thinking. With the "right/wrong" or "healthy/unhealthy" thinking, there is no learning, exploring, or expanding, it's a sad place.

The binary arguments sound like this: "if someone is not anti-porn it must mean they are pro-porn". But the subject of pornography is not so simple, and indeed, it deserves more nuanced thinking. I think it is crucial to stay in the grey areas to allow questioning and the expanding of thinking to occur.

It is OK to love porn and it is OK to hate it. The porn lovers are not sexier people and the porn haters are not boring people. Whatever people want to do in their private life with porn is up to them and their values. When we have debates about it, I think it is important to be as neutral as possible, hang out in the grey areas, perhaps allow ourselves to be a little uncomfortable, and gain greater awareness of the pros and cons of porn, not just one or the other. It is within that neutral place that we can genuinely be curious about it.

Pros:
1. There is now a vast body of good research in sexology, psychology, psychiatry, and sociology that keeps replicating the same results: pornography does not *cause* sexual problems or mental health problems.
2. Pornography does not *cause* misogyny. Misogyny predates online porn by centuries.
3. Pornography can enhance people's sex lives if the people in the relationship share the same values about it.
4. LGBTQ+ people and disabled people do not have representations of their romantic and erotic lives in the media, leaving them further erotically marginalised. Porn for the LGBTQ+ people and disabled people can be a good source of visibility on how people of the same gender can interact erotically, or how disabled people can have fulfilling sex. Porn can be a platform of sexual validation and freedom.

You can find a collection of those research on this website: https://porn-science.com

Cons:

1. Although pornography doesn't cause misogyny, it can collude with it. Mainstream cisgender heterosexual porn can be ghastly. The male performers look bored, the female performers look in pain having anal sex with no lube. It's like Dom/sub play gone terribly wrong … The oral sex scenes aren't any better; men missing the clitoris completely while women fake screaming as though they had the best orgasm of their life … Women choking on the penis so hard you can tell it is hurting them. All of these porn scenes send terrible messages of the sexual expectations of men and women.

2. The performer's bodies are unrealistic, with perfectly designed and hairless vulvas, larger than average penises, making viewers feel bad about their bodies.

3. It is obvious that it is adult entertainment made by men who don't know much about sexual health for the viewing pleasure of other men who also have poor sex education. It's no surprise there are a large number of women coming to therapy complaining that their male sexual partners are too aggressive and trying to be like a porn star.

Staying in the grey areas means that we should not ignore the problems with porn but we should not demonise it either. Instead, we can question and reflect. For example, an uncomfortable question is what makes mainstream heterosexual porn so misogynistic? Pornography has never wanted to be sex education nor altruistic. Given that it is a profit-making industry, it responds to demand. So, if the demand is for misogynistic porn, does it mean that the bigger issue is how men become so? If men were raised with less strict ideas of masculinity and without overt or covert sexist ideas in the first place, would they demand such porn? The research in pornography indicates that people don't watch online contents they find morally wrong, they usually click away within seconds (Ley, 2016), which means that people watching that kind of mainstream misogynistic porn may actually like the idea of watching such content in the first place. While we know from research that porn does not cause misogyny, it can certainly maintain it. Demonising porn for men's sexual behaviours may be a red herring in order to avoid the more unsettling problem: how do we collude with society's intrinsic misogyny when raising our boys? Indeed, challenging misogyny and changing some core beliefs of masculinity in our society is a much bigger job than simply pointing the finger at porn.

The poor sex education on boundaries, consent, pleasure, and good, equal relationships is the real problem, whether we like porn or not. In fact, distorted messages about consent, gender roles, and relationships are sprinkled all over our most adored Disney cartoons, and we allow all our children to watch them.

PORNOGRAPHY MYTHS

There are many myths about pornography being bad for our society. Let's de-mystify the most common ones.

Sexual crimes

David Ley (2016) asserts that sexual crimes are lower in countries where porn is more available. Pornography may offer adults a space to satisfy their erotic curiosity safely. Most people masturbate to pornography so it can also be a way to discharge some sexual tension. In countries (or cultures) where porn is banned, erotic curiosity and sexual energy have much fewer spaces to be explored, thus encouraging people to demand it from other people, which may be the motivation for sexual assault. Morever, Nelson and Rothman (2020) state

> pornography itself is not a crisis. The movement to declare pornography a public health crisis is rooted in an ideology that is antithetical to many core values of public health promotion and is a political stunt, not reflective of best available evidence.

Objectification

This is a term describing making a person an object of sexual desire and gratification. In Chapter 4, I explained that the research on sexual fantasies by Lehmiller (2018) indicate that men and women objectify to connect to their erotic aliveness. Women objectifying men is perceived as less problematic and less taboo, whereas men objectifying women is deemed more dangerous. If the objectification is done in a way that makes the objectified person uncomfortable, it is definitely not good. But much objectification may be harmless. Objectification is a loaded word but it is important to be balanced about it.

Relationship problems

As explained earlier, pornography does not *cause* relationship problems per se. The relationship problems come from a conflict in values. For example, a person who is vegan because of strong values of animal rights might have frequent conflicts if they are in a relationship with someone who loves meat and is unwilling to change their dietary habits. It is also common that people who have different values on politics, money, parenting, or religion from their partner(s) have more conflicts with them than those who share the same values. The same goes for pornography. It is not the pornography itself that is the problem, it is what people think about it. If people in a relationship have the same positive values about watching pornography, it can actually be good for their sex lives. Staley and Prause (2013) found that porn can increase people's desire to be close to their current partner.

Equally, it won't do harm to relationships if the people in the relationship have the same negative values about pornography. If they dislike it, they won't watch it, and they won't have conflicts about it. In my clinic, I often notice that people who have conflicts about pornography have not had the explicit conversation about their porn values when they first met, assuming that they might think and feel the same about it, or ignoring the uncomfortable conversation. Without the explicit conversation, it's impossible to carefully select a partner who shares the same values about porn. Gay men tend to have less conflicts about their partner(s) watching porn because they are usually more open about their porn use and therefore they tend to have more similar values about it.

It is common for cisgender men to feel insecure if their cisgender female partner buys a sex toy (fearing that the sex toy will replace their penis) just as it is common that cisgender women can feel insecure about their cisgender male partner watching pornography.

Often, women may think that if their partner watches porn featuring women with big breasts and they happen to have smaller breasts, it means that their partner doesn't like their breasts and that they secretly want to have sex with someone who has bigger breasts. This is a common insecurity that doesn't translate in reality. As I explained earlier, fantasies are not necessarily linked to sexual behaviours in real life, and most people think about their partners more than they do about porn performers. If people feel insecure in their relationships, it is better to learn to express those insecurities (and values) rather than blaming their partner for watching porn, because unresolved insecurities often remain with or without partners watching porn.

Unreliable erections

There is a pervasive fear, especially among young men, that their porn use causes erectile dysfunction (ED). This fear is fuelled by much of the "porn panic" noise, which does not have much scientific evidence. Jacobs et al. (2021) looked into this problem and found that there *might* be a link with people who have problematic use of porn. The issue with this is that the scientific communities haven't yet agreed on what constitutes "problematic use", and what is the difference between "problematic" and "frequent" because those assessments are so subjective. The study states:

> Frequency of pornography use did not seem to have an important impact on the occurrence of ED. Only when consuming pornography for more than 30 minutes in a row was the frequency of ED slightly higher, but most participants (89%) do not consume pornography for more than 30 minutes.

The study also found no evidence to support that masturbation frequency has an effect on ED.

The term PIED (porn-induced erectile dysfunction) has largely been disproved in scientific studies and there are no recognised diagnostic criteria for it because of the lack of evidence (Landripet and Štulhofer, 2015; Prause and Pfaus, 2015; Berger et al., 2019; Grubbs and Gola, 2019). Moreover, Rowland et al. (2021) showed that the quality of erections are better in solo sex than in partnered sex, even when there is not a dysfunction. People who have better erections with porn and less good ones with their partner(s) might worry that it is because of porn, when, in fact, it is normal. Macdowall et al. (2021) find that more masturbation is associated with higher testosterone, not lower. This is contrary to some anti-porn/anti-masturbation forums claiming that semen retention (also called "reboot") is good for men's sex lives. In fact, it appears that the opposite happens. More testosterone is also associated with better erections, which further disproves the PIED myth.

THE USE OF PORNOGRAPHY

I wrote earlier about the problematic use of pornography but now that I have explained the basic ins and outs of pornography (pun intended), I hope you can begin to understand how porn is used and how it is not problematic for many people. Pornography is mostly used for sexual pleasure and masturbation. It is used for a good quality time of solo sex. It can also be used for soothing after a stressful day, or for celebration after a great day. All of these different ways of using pornography are not problematic. The frequency is also not problematic. Some use it every day, while others use it once a month, it doesn't matter. Heterosexual people may watch gay porn. Gay people may watch heterosexual porn. Many people are fond of porn with transgender people. All of these do not necessarily present a problem.

In Chapter 3, I wrote about digisexuality. Some people prefer to engage with pornography as their primary way to meet their sexual satisfaction. It does not classify as a problem. It can be a normative way to use porn for digisexual people.

Some people with disabilities may not feel comfortable or may not be able to have sex with other people, so watching porn and masturbating (or cybersex) may be their primary way to have a fulfilling sex life.

The main benefit of not getting caught in the "porn panic" noise is that we can accept that people will have different attractions to porn, people use it for different reasons. Embracing the idea that some people love porn and some hate it, and nobody has to persuade anyone else to either love it or hate it, is making a commitment to people's fundamental rights to sexual pleasure and people's autonomy.

ETHICAL PORN

The best solution to the problems of the mainstream porn industry (misogyny and potential exploitation of their performers) is to access ethical porn instead.

Ethical porn, also called "fair trade porn" or "feminist porn", is sex-positive pornography made respectfully and consensually with no exploitation, where performers have full rights to only do what they are comfortable to do.

Ethical porn tends to show more realistic and everyday sex which includes performers of all body types, all genders, all sexual orientations, all legal sexual practices, a wide variety of genitals and diverse relationships including queer relationships. Ethical porn is made for everyone to enjoy, it is much more inclusive. However, it is not accessible for free. As adult entertainment, like all other entertainment, I think it is a good thing to pay for it.

Ethical porn is getting more buzz and attention, so it is now tempting for porn companies to put the label of ethical porn on their products while not employing the philosophy of it. As responsible consumers, it is worth checking the company's policies and ethos before engaging in it. If you like some performers you see in ethical porn, it can be a good idea to follow them on social media, which gives them a voice and checks their particular views and opinions about the companies they work with. When people find an ethical porn company that fits with their values, they can support it by maintaining a paid membership to it, just like supporting a small, local business.

REVENGE PORN

Revenge porn is sharing explicit images or films on public platforms or with a selected group of people without the consent of the people in those images or films. It is called revenge porn because this is usually done in the context of hurting someone after a break-up. Revenge porn is illegal (see Chapter 9). Filming and taking explicit sexual pictures has become very common. It is very important for the public to have a better understanding of the consequences of sending an explicit picture to someone they don't know well, or the potential risk of filming sexual content when in a relationship.

SUMMARY

Whether you love or hate porn, it is an emotive subject shrouded in much "porn panic" noise that makes the topic difficult to navigate. It is confusing to know what is problematic porn use and what is not, and it brings insecurities that motivate people to impose their views on others about it. It is, however, important to embrace people's rights to sexual pleasure and autonomy, and to accept that people have different views and values about it. If people want to avoid having a conflict with their partner(s) about porn, it is a good idea to make sure they have explicit conversations early in their relationship to check each other's values about it. For the people who love porn, why not pay for it with ethical porn, like paying for other entertainment?

Reflective questions:

1 What are your automatic thoughts and feelings about porn?

2 If you love or hate porn, do you know what information this is based on?

3 Is there anything about this chapter that made you uncomfortable or angry? Do you know why?

4 What were the values that you believed to be true or "facts" before reading this chapter? What do you think now?

FURTHER READING

Monogamy with Benefits. How Porn Enriches Our Relationship, by Geri and Jay Hart. (2015).

Ethical Porn for Dicks. A Man's Guide To Responsible Viewing Pleasure, by David J. Ley, PhD (2016).

Porn Panic. Sex and Censorship in the UK, by Jerry Barnett (2016).

REFERENCES

American Psychiatric Association (2013). *Diagnostic and Statistical Manual of Mental Health Disorders*, Fifth Edition (DSM-5). American Psychiatric Publishing. Arlington, VA.

Barnett, J. (2016). *Porn Panic! Sex and Censorship in the UK*. Zero Books. Alresford, Hants.

Berger, J.H., Kehoe, J.E., Doan, A.P., Crain, D.S., Klam, W.P., Marshall, M.T., & Christman, M.S. (2019). Survey of Sexual Function and Pornography. *Military Medicine*, Dec 1, 184(11–12), 731–737. doi:10.1093/milmed/usz079. PMID: 31132108.

Binnie, J., & Reavy, P. (2020). Development and Implications of Pornography Use: A Narrative Review. *Sexual and Relationship Therapy*, 35(2), 178–194.

Chakrabarti, N., Chopra, V.K., & Sinha, V.K. (2002). Masturbatory Guilt Leading to Severe Depression and Erectile Dysfunction. *Journal of Sex & Marital Therapy*, 28, 285–287. Brunner-Routledge.

Charig, R., Moghaddam N.G., Dawson, D.L., Merdian, H.L., & Das Nair, R. (2020). A lack of association between online pornography exposure, sexual functioning, and mental well-being. *Sexual and Relationship Therapy*, 35(2), 258281. doi:10.1080/14681994.2020.1727874

Chasioti, D., & Binnie, J. (2021). Exploring the Etiological Pathways of Problematic Pornography Use in NoFap/PornFree Rebooting Communities: A Critical Narrative Analysis of Internet Forum Data. *Archives of Sexual Behavior*, 50, 2227–2243. doi:10.1007/s10508-021-01930-z

Grubbs, J.B., & Gola, M. (2019). Is Pornography Use Related to Erectile Functioning? Results from Cross-Sectional and Latent Growth Curve Analyses. *The Journal of Sexual Medicine*, 16(1), 111–125.

Grubbs, J.B., Hoagland, K.C., Lee, B.N., Grant, J.T., Davison, P., Reid, R.C., & Kraus, S.W. (2020a). Sexual Addiction 25 Years On: A Systematic and Methodological Review of Empirical Literature and an Agenda for Future Research. *Clinical Psychology Review*, Dec, 82, 101925. doi:10.1016/j.cpr.2020.101925

Grubbs, J.B., Kraus, S.W., Perry, S.L., Lewczuk, K., & Gola, M. (2020b). Moral Incongruence and Compulsive Sexual Behavior: Results from Cross-Sectional Interactions and Parallel Growth Curve Analyses. *Journal of Abnormal Psychology*, 129(3), 266–278. doi:10.1037/abn0000501

International Classification of Diseases. Eleventh revision (2019). 11th Revision. (ICD-11). World Health Organization (WHO). [Available Online]: https://icd.who.int/en

Jacobs, T., Geysemans, B., Van Hal, G., Glazemakers, I., Fog-Poulsen, K., Vermandel, A., De Wachter, S., & De Win, G. (2021). Associations Between Online Pornography Consumption and Sexual Dysfunction in Young Men:

Multivariate Analysis Based on an International Web-Based Survey. *JMIR Public Health Surveill*, Oct 21, 7(10), e32542. doi:10.2196/32542. PMID: 34534092; PMCID: PMC8569536.

Kohut, T., Fisher, W.A., & Campbell, L. (2017). Perceived Effects of Pornography on the Couple Relationship: Initial Findings of Open-Ended, Participant-Informed, "Bottom-Up" Research. *Archives of Sexual Behavior*, Feb, 46(2), 585–602. doi:10.1007/s10508-016-0783-6. Epub 2016 Jul 8. Erratum in: Arch Sex Behav. 2017 Feb; 46(2):603. PMID: 27393037.

Landripet, I., & Štulhofer, A. (2015). Is Pornography Use Associated with Sexual Difficulties and Dysfunctions Among Younger Heterosexual Men? *The Journal of Sexual Medicine*, 12(5), 1136–1139.

Lehmiller, J. (2018). *Tell Me What You Want. The Science of Sexual Desire and How It Can Help You Improve Your Sex Life*. Robinson. Da Capo Press. New York.

Ley, D. (2016). *Ethical Porn for Dicks. A man's Guide to Responsible Viewing Pleasure*. ThreeL Media. Berkeley, California.

Macdowall, W.G., Clifton, S., Palmer, M.J., Tanton, C., Copas, A.J., Lee, D.M., Mitchell, K.R., Mercer, C.H., Sonnenberg, P., Johnson A.M., & Wellings, K. (2021). Salivary Testosterone and Sexual Function and Behavior in Men and Women: Findings from the Third British National Survey of Sexual Attitudes and Lifestyles (Natsal-3), *The Journal of Sex Research*. doi:10.1080/00224499.2021.1968327

McKee, A., Byron, P., Litsou, K., & Ingham, R. (2020). An Interdisciplinary Definition of Pornography: Results from a Global Delphi Panel. *Archives of Sexual Behavior*, 49, 1085–1091. doi:10.1007/s10508-019-01554-4

Nelson, K.M., & Rothman, E.F. (2020). Should Public Health Professionals Consider Pornography a Public Health Crisis? *American Journal of Public Health*, Feb 1, 110(2), 151–153. doi:10.2105/AJPH.2019.305498

Neves, S. (2021). *Compulsive Sexual Behaviours. A Psycho-Sexual Treatment Guide for Clinicians*. Routledge. Abingdon, Oxon.

Perry, S.L. (2020). Is the Link Between Pornography Use and Relational Happiness Really More About Masturbation? Results from Two National Surveys. *The Journal of Sex Research*, 57(1), 64–76, doi:10.1080/00224499.2018.1556772

Prause, N., & Pfaus, J. (2015). Viewing Sexual Stimuli Associated with Greater Sexual Responsiveness, Not Erectile Dysfunction. *Sexual Medicine*, 3(2), 90–98.

Przybylski, A. (2021). Why Scientists Don't Actually Know if Social Media Media is Bad for You. *BBC Science Focus Magazine*, May. [Available Online]: https://www.sciencefocus.com/future-technology/why-scientists-dont-actually-know-if-social-media-is-bad-for-you/

Rothschild, B. (2021). *Revolutionizing Trauma Treatment. Stabilization, Safety, & Nervous System Balance*. W.W. Norton & Company, Inc. New York.

Rowland, D.L., Hamilton, B.D., Bacys, K.R., & Hevesi, K. (2021). Sexual Response Differs during Partnered Sex and Masturbation in Men With and Without Sexual Dysfunction: Implications for Treatment. *The Journal of Sexual Medicine*, Nov, 18(11), 1835–1842. doi:10.1016/j.jsxm.2021.09.005. Epub 2021 Oct 7. PMID: 34627718.

Staley, C., & Prause, N. (2013). Erotica Viewing Effects On Intimate Relationships and Self/Partner Evaluations. *Archives of Sexual Behavior*, 42(4), 615–624.

RELATIONSHIPS

The term "relationship" encapsulates a wide range of human connections from intimate to distant, functional to dysfunctional, romantic to professional, sexual to platonic. Some can be positive relationships and others can be damaging or toxic.

In this book, we are going to focus on intimate relationships in the context of romantic and sexual aspects of relating, but, first, I would like to offer a broader view of relationships. When we speak of relationships we may refer to:

1. *Romantic relationships* including dating, being in love, being in a relationship with one or several people whom you have a romantic attraction to. It may mean being in a civil partnership or married. It may or may not include sexual contact/attraction.
2. *Sexual relationships* including dating and having sexual contact with one or more people. It may involve an ongoing sexual relationship with or without romantic attraction, or it may also describe a one-off sexual encounter.
3. *Family relationships* including any people connected to a family network either biologically, by adoption, or by marriage. Some of these relationships may be close or distant, loving and caring, damaging or neutral. They include parent/children relationships, siblings, cousins, aunts, uncles, family-in-law, and pets!
4. *Friendships* including people who like to be around each other. They can be peers, loving and caring relationships without romantic or sexual attraction. They can be people sharing a hobby, common interests, or goals. Friends are people who are supportive. Some close friendships may also be referred to

DOI: 10.4324/9781003276913-9

as "family of choice" (especially for people from LGBTQ+ communities).

5. *Online relationships* including any relationships that are conducted entirely online. These relationships can be peers, friendships, romantic, or sexual relationships.

6. *Acquaintances* including people who are on the periphery of social networks but who don't hold much importance in a person's life.

7. *Work relationships/colleagues* including people linked with work. Some may be peers, some can hold a power dynamic of employer-employee. Some collegial relationships develop into friendships, and some may become romantic or sexual. Some work relationships can be negative or toxic and others can become acquaintances.

8. *Location-based relationships* including relationships that happen solely based on locations, where people live. These relationships can be tenant-landlord, neighbours, or flatmates. Some may become friendships; some develop into a romantic or sexual relationship. Some may become damaging, toxic, or neutral.

9. *Teacher–student relationships* are a particular type of relationship that have the power dynamic of one teaching the other. These relationships usually have strict boundaries, when dual relationships such as friendships, romantic, or sexual relationships are prohibited.

10. *Therapist-client relationships* are another particular type of relationship that exists solely for the therapeutic benefit of the client. This type of relationship has a one-way direction of care, from therapist to client, which is not reciprocated. This relationship has strict boundaries. Friendships, romantic, or sexual relationships are prohibited. Although this relationship is a one-way system, it is nevertheless a strong and connected relationship in which much healing happens.

11. *Community group or faith-based group relationships* including a group of people gathering for a common pursuit, whether it is a community or faith-based one. Some of these relationships may become peers, friendships, romantic, or sexual, or they may develop into negative and toxic ones. Some of the dynamics within the group can be complex and there usually are multiple levels of quality of connections between various members of the group.

FRIENDSHIPS

One of the most crucial relationships that we have as human beings is friendship. Some friendships are brief, some are lifelong; nevertheless, they form an important part of our relational field both in terms of intimacy and support. For example, there are some things that people feel more comfortable sharing with a close friend than with the person they are in a romantic and sexual relationship with. In our society, we hold sexual and romantic relationships with so much importance that we tend to forget about paying enough attention to friendships. Some people say: "My partner is my best friend", yet there are some clear differences between friendships and romantic relationships, but both should be viewed as equally important, rather than one trumping the other. Indeed, some friendships suffer when one becomes involved in a romantic relationship, which leaves no more space for that friendship.

Friendships form the important web of human connection that we need in order to live a good and balanced life. Even though much support can be found in a romantic relationship, one romantic relationship may not be enough to meet all the relational and emotional needs of a person. Multiple partnered relationships can sometimes meet a wider range of needs, but, even so, there are some sensitive parts of oneself that can only be met in a friendship where there is no romantic or sexual attraction, but plenty of love and care. Some people experience their friendships as a place where there is the most unconditional positive regard.

Many people don't feel able to speak to their romantic and sexual partner(s) about some important parts of themselves, for example, insecurities, anxieties, longings, or existential wonderings, because of a worry that they may burden their partners. It's easier to bring up some of those conversations with close friends or a therapist.

Esther Perel (2006) speaks of the pressure that we put on our romantic and sexual relationship. Couples who live in isolation, far away from their support systems, may expect so much from one person (in the case of a monogamous relationship) or a handful of people (in polyamorous relationships), but a romantic and sexual system is not enough for us all to thrive, we need a "tribe" – whether it means family, friendships, or peers.

I love the concept of a "tribe". It is a group of people with whom we feel completely relaxed and trusting. It feels like home.

A romantic and sexual partner may or may not be part of that tribe. The tribe is sometimes the place to go to for a respite from a romantic and sexual relationship. It is particularly important for people of minority communities to find their tribe so that they can have a respite from the rest of the world that might not understand them or accept them so well.

The tribe makes up a big part of a person's "Inner Circle" of their human connections. Romantic and sexual partner(s) may also be part of the Inner Circle but could be separate from the tribe.

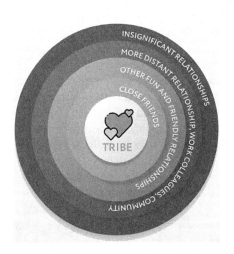

Figure 8.1   Relationship Circles

INTIMACY

When we think of intimacy, we often make the mistake of equating it to sexual intimacy, but the ultimate meaning of intimacy is a connection where one feels truly and authentically seen ("Into-Me-You-See"). The feeling of being seen, heard, and understood in a meaningful way is the essence of well-being and contentment. Such intimacy is possible within romantic and sexual relationships but not solely. It can also happen with close friendships and it is one of the healing agents of therapy, so it is often found in the therapist–client relationship.

Equally, intimacy can be spontaneous and temporary as it can happen within the short relationship of a one-off sexual encounter. These fleeting moments are often dismissed and not considered as intimate, but some people report that they felt truly seen within the throes of erotic passion with a stranger. These kinds of encounters are ones that people remember forever because they are meaningful moments.

INTIMATE RELATIONSHIPS: ROMANTIC AND SEXUAL RELATIONSHIPS

When looking at all the possible types of relationships mentioned above, we can see how many of them have the potential to become romantic or sexual ones. Let us look at intimate relationships in the context of romantic and sexual attraction.

Monogamy refers to being in a romantic and/or sexual relationship with one other person at any given time. People who choose monogamy don't often talk about it explicitly, which is a mistake because monogamy means different things to different people. Assuming that your definition of monogamy is the same as your partner's may cause some issues. For some people, monogamy means exclusivity in romantic and sexual contact, but it is OK to flirt with other people. For some, it might be OK to watch pornography and masturbate, for others this is unacceptable. For some, sexting is OK as long as there is no intention of meeting other people. Some people even consider monogamy a romantic exclusivity but not necessarily a sexual one. Monogamy is the commitment of prioritising one person over the rest, but the nature of those priorities may vary greatly from one monogamous couple to the next.

Monogamish is a term coined by Dan Savage (2005) which means a relationship that is monogamous most of the time with occasional intimate/sexual contacts outside of the primary relationship. It may be a monogamous couple who agree that once a year (a birthday, for example) each will have a weekend away separately and indulge in a sexual experience without their partner. Some couples have the rule of "don't ask, don't tell" while others enjoy sharing their weekend erotic tales with each other. Some monogamish couples agree on their occasional sexual indulgence to be more than once a year, for example, for some, it may be once a month. The point is that these couples are monogamous most of the time, and everything is agreed upon and consensual.

CNM stands for consensual non-monogamy. It is also called *ENM* (ethical non-monogamy). These terms are often used interchangeably. Defining consensual non-monogamy or ethical non-monogamy is tricky as these are value-based so the meanings are subjective. Some cultures or religious communities do not agree that non-monogamy can be ethical. For other communities, the imposition of monogamy may feel oppressive. As a general definition, consensual non-monogamy and ethical non-monogamy refer to relationships that allow romantic and/or sexual contact with more than one person at a time. The consensual and ethical element means that these relationships are fully agreed upon by all the people involved intimately in these relationships. If some information is withdrawn that make full informed consent impossible, the non-monogamous relationships are not ethical nor consensual. Some CNM and ENM have different boundaries depending on what is agreed upon. For some, there is a romantic boundary, for example sex with multiple partners is allowed but not romantic relationships. For others, having friendships or romantic relationships with multiple people is allowed. People enjoying CNM often describe the feeling of *compersion*, which is the feeling of joy at seeing or hearing the sexual and/or romantic happiness their partners have with other people. It is being happy for their partner's happiness, which, for some, is deemed as the essential ingredient of love.

Polyamory refers to loving more than one person at any given time. Polyamory often includes sexual relationships with multiple partners but not always. Just like CNM, the boundaries of polyamorous relationships have to be fully agreed upon by all the people involved for full, informed consent to engage in these relationships. One polyamorous system varies greatly from another depending on the agreements. Some polyamorous people describe their relationship style as an "orientation" while others want to pursue it as a "lifestyle choice" (Fern, 2020).

Polyfidelity means a closed group of people who are in CNM relationships with each other only; they all know each other and the introduction of strangers or new people in the system is forbidden. Some of these systems can be called "throuple" (sometimes spelt "thruple", a relationship with three people, also known as *menage à trois*). Some systems go beyond threesomes into four or more.

V relationships refer to one person in a relationship with two different partners that are not in relationships with each other, thus creating a V-shaped relationship. In some V relationships, the two partners making the "V" may be strangers to each other, but in some others, they may know each other and even be close friends with each other, but without any romantic or sexual contact. As with all relationships, an ethical V relationship is when all partners involved are aware and agree on the V relationship.

Relationship Anarchy (RA), also called "relationship queer", is an attitude to relationships that questions and challenges the perception that romantic relationships are more important than other relationships. The philosophy of RA is the understanding that each relationship is unique and equally important, whether sexual, romantic, or otherwise, and evolves organically into different dimensions. People who are in RA believe in the abundance of love that doesn't need to be limited and many different types of romantic and sexual relationships can happen at any given time.

Polygamy describes being married to multiple spouses. It is currently not legal in the UK and in other Western countries but is legally practiced in some other cultures. However, the most common set-up is polygyny, one man married to multiple wives, and the least popular is polyandry, one woman married to multiple husbands, which is a reflection of worldwide gender bias and sexism.

Friends with benefits (FWB) is self-explanatory. It refers to friendships that allow an opportunity for sexual contact with each other, either occasionally or frequently. These relationships are fully agreed upon.

Swinging is the practice of couples (usually ones that identify themselves as monogamous) who occasionally engage in sexual activities with other couples or single people. Those couples often do this by going to specific swingers' clubs or sometimes parties organised privately in people's homes (see Chapter 6).

ATTACHMENT STYLES

John Bowlby (1969, 1973, 1980), the father of attachment theory, made a significant contribution to psychology in better understanding how human beings attach to others. Attachment theory is complex, so I won't do it justice here, but I want to offer an overview of it because it is important in the context of intimate relationships. Broadly, it is thought that people have four different attachment styles: secure, anxious, avoidant, or disorganised attachments. These describe how people attach to others, based on their first experiences of attachment, how they attached to their parents or primary care givers. For example, if parents placed conditions on their love for their children, such as "we love you when you have good grades", the child is likely to develop an anxious attachment style when they might worry as adults that their partners could stop loving them as soon as they're not at their best.

Secure attachment

People who are secure in their attachments feel comfortable in their relationships. They often had a good and calm childhood when they felt consistently loved by their parents. They are happy to show their emotions and share their thoughts and feelings with their partner(s). When they fall in love, they can easily commit to the relationship(s) without much anxiety. They are clear about their boundaries and what they want in their relationships. They tend to have good self-esteem. They feel safe in their relationships and they can tolerate their partner's autonomy. They trust people easily and don't second guess what people say. In the language of Transactional Analysis (Stewart and Joines, 1987), people with a secure attachment style hold the core belief that: "I'm OK – you're OK".

Anxious attachment

People who anxiously attach usually have poor self-esteem. They often think that they are not good enough. They believe that they have to be perfect or always useful in order to keep the love of their partner(s). They often interpret communication with others as people criticising them even when they aren't. They often worry that their partner(s) will leave them because they can find a better person somewhere else, which leaves them in a state of hypervigilance, scanning their partner's behaviours, facial expressions, and tone of voice to decipher whether their partner(s) love them. Hypervigilance is a common strategy children adopt when they grow up in a volatile household, for example when they don't know if their parents will be in a good mood or not. People who have anxious attachment styles often report growing up in households where moods were changeable frequently, leaving a sense of unpredictability, never knowing what would happen next. They usually second-guess their partner(s) and they don't trust their partner(s) being truthful when they compliment them. In fact, they find it hard to receive compliments or praise, yet they consistently seek reassurance from others that they're liked and loved. They are very sensitive to rejections. Their core belief is: "I'm not OK – you're OK".

Avoidant attachment

People with avoidant attachment also have poor self-esteem. They value their autonomy very highly and they think that nobody can take care of them so they need to look after themselves. They don't like it when people come too close to them without appropriate warning. They can easily feel suffocated and perceive their partner(s) as being intrusive of their private space. They will often perceive people who don't have an avoidant attachment style as needy. The more people want to be around them, the more they'll want to move away from them. People who have avoidant attachment styles usually grow up in households where parents were intrusive with poor boundaries, for example an overbearing parent, walking in their bedroom without knocking, or having overly strict house rules imposed on them. Some people describe having endured a childhood with domestic abuse. Their core belief is: "I'm OK – you're not OK".

Disorganised attachment

People with a disorganised attachment usually are people who have endured severe trauma in childhood, particularly severe neglect from parents or primary care givers. They perceive the world as a dangerous place where nobody can be trusted. Their main goal is to survive the inhospitable environment of relating with other human beings so they tend to prioritise their needs over others. They are afraid of closeness and intimacy in relationships. They cannot tolerate vulnerability. They may feel angry and respond aggressively when people challenge them. They can sometimes struggle to feel empathy for others when they think they're misunderstood. They do not like to discuss boundaries in relationships because they don't want to attach in the first place; however, they might also want to feel love and warmth from others, which makes their attachment style disorganised, or, in other words, confusing. They struggle with emotional regulation and their mood can be unpredictable. Their core belief Is, "I'm not OK – you're not OK".

Another lens that we can explore attachments is through the dimensions of seeking proximity and anxiety of abandonment. How much proximity do we like to maintain with the people we're in a relationship with? How much anxiety do we feel at the possibility to be abandoned by the people we're in a relationship with? What is the relationship between those two dimensions of seeking proximity and anxiety of abandonment?

> *Secure*: people who want proximity and who are low in anxiety of abandonment.
> *Preoccupied*: people who want proximity and who are high in anxiety of abandonment.
> *Fearful*: people who don't want proximity and who are high in anxiety of abandonment.
> *Dismissive*: people who don't want proximity and who are low in anxiety of abandonment.

MONONORMATIVITY

Mononormativity is the assumption that monogamy is the "gold standard", or the "normal" and everything else is "weird" or "abnormal" (Barker, 2018a). It is important to note that the four attachment styles, explained above, are not synonyms for relationship diversities. From a mononormative point of view, it can be easy to automatically assume that someone in an open relationship is a person who can't securely attach to one other person. People who are not in relationships do not necessarily have a disorganised/dismissive attachment style, just the same way that people in a happy monogamous relationship are not the hallmark of secure attachments.

Attachment theory and the various attachment styles are not meant to be knowledge to pathologise people and their non-monogamous relationships. Attachment theories are useful for exploring how people attach based on their first attachments. The attachment patterns of some people may be because of their neurodiversity. Some disabled people may appear to have an anxious/preoccupied attachment style when, in fact, they are being more careful when meeting other people due to the very real possibility of being misunderstood or criticised. People from marginalised communities may appear to dislike proximity seeking, which is their functional strategies to stay safe. Exploration is curiosity. Assumption is a lack of curiosity.

MODERN UNDERSTANDING OF ATTACHMENTS

Figuring out our attachment style is not a life sentence nor is it relevant to all the situations in our life. One person may have diverse attachment styles depending on the situation. For example, people don't attach to potential lovers the same way as they may attach to friends or family members. Some people can have an anxious/preoccupied attachment with their boss because of the power dynamics and they might feel intimidated by them, but might have a secure attachment with their intimate partner(s). Some can have an avoidant/dismissive attachment with their neighbours because they have nothing in common but can attach securely with friends. Attachment styles are not fixed. Although we learn how to attach from our childhood, we can also change our attachment patterns by healing the wounds of childhood, raising our self-esteem and self-worth, and reconfiguring where we stand in relationships. This is a process that can be facilitated by therapy.

Jessica Fern (2020) writes:

> Attachment styles are *not* static! If you experienced an insecurely attached childhood you can still go on to have healthy securely attached adult relationships, experiencing what is called an *earned secure attachment*. Your attachment styles are survival adaptations to your environment and since they were learned, they can also be unlearned.

(2020, pp. 25–26)

Indeed, as humans, we are relational beings. It means that we can be deeply wounded in cold, abusive or toxic relationships, and, by the same process of relating, we can heal and thrive in warm, loving, and caring relationships.

As the attachment theories have developed, I would like to challenge the idea of "co-dependency". Many people report not expressing their needs in relationships because they're afraid to sound "too needy". When someone expresses a need at an inconvenient time, it is easy to label that person "needy". I would like to encourage people to reclaim the word "needy" because as human beings we have needs. We are very different from one another but we also have the universal need for food, sleep, shelter, touch, warmth, connections and love. Without those things, we are likely to die prematurely (or not live very well).

Being in any relationship is a commitment to knowing our needs and to take our partners' needs into consideration and behave accordingly. No matter what type of relationships we have, what we do and say will have an impact on our partner(s) and vice versa.

It is OK to rely on some of our partner's strengths to complement areas of life that are a weakness for us. That is not a sign of co-dependency. For example, one who loves cooking may cook every day for the one who doesn't enjoy cooking. A good relationship isn't necessarily one where all the chores are equally divided. A good relationship is when all the chores and obligations are properly discussed and teamwork has been fully agreed upon. Relationships need a certain amount of flexibility and adaptation. Relationships that may appear "co-dependent" might be great safe spaces for the people in these relationships, and co-dependency is only a judgement from people outside of the relationship looking in. Is it so bad that one person doesn't want to live on when their loved one dies? Is it wrong for people to rely on someone else for some things? Some people would hate to be in those kinds of relationships, which is fair enough, but others might love it. Let's not use blanket labels that are loaded with implied dysfunction.

It can sometimes be a struggle to figure out what we want and what we need in relationships. There is a pervasive myth that intimate relationships should meet all of one's needs, and happiness can only be reached when that happens. Many feel bad about their relationships not because of inadequate partner(s) but because of a belief that they're not getting what they *should* deserve in a relationship. If we want our partner(s) to meet some of our needs, we should be explicit about them because our partner's loving connection won't give them the superpower of reading our minds.

The concept of "need" is loaded and can encourage judgements rather than validating people's autonomy in choosing the people they want to share their life with. When Fernando first introduced his new partner Giovanna to his family, there was some tension. Giovanna was a wheelchair user and had chronic fatigue (which was perceived as laziness). As she didn't work, Fernando's parents were suspicious of her because they thought she would take advantage of him. When they found out that she came from a rich family and had inherited enough money to live comfortably as a financially independent woman for the rest of her life, Fernando's parents became very friendly with her. However, when Giovanna helped Fernando financially with starting his own business, her friends thought that Fernando was in the relationship to take advantage of her. All along, the actual genuine love between a disabled person and a non-disabled person was unseen and even dismissed because people's unfounded judgements got in the way.

THE PLANETARY SYSTEM OF RELATIONSHIPS

Schnarch (2009) writes about "differentiation", a term describing our self-awareness within relationships, how our emotions and behaviours are influenced by the moving in-between "individuality" and "togetherness". Indeed, the better we know ourselves the more aware we can be about how we stand in relationships, the diverse roles we take, what makes us thrive or shrink, how we influence or are influenced by others, and what behaviours we adopt to give and receive love, but also to protect ourselves.

A relationship is the space in-between two people (for a couple) or more (for multiple partnered relationships). The space in-between is made of what the people involved in the relationship put in it. For example, if people put in the space coldness and stress, the relationship is likely to feel cold and stressful. If people put in warmth and care, the relationship will feel warm and caring. That "temperature" of the space can change instantly depending on what the people put in it at any given time. For example, if one puts in warmth they contribute to the warmth of the relationship, but if a moment later that same person becomes stressed because they received an unpleasant email, the space can instantly change from warm to stressed. The space is indeed responsive to what the people feel, say, behave, or how they invest in the relationship.

If there is much investment in care and trust, the relationship space builds a strong connection. Such relationships can sustain temporary moments of stress, coldness, or anger. If there isn't much investment in the relationship, it can be weak and can wobble very easily in moments of stress.

While the relationship is the co-created space in-between the people in it, the other important spaces are the individual spaces of each person in the relationship, being their own world.

I'm a fan of cosmology. I like to conceptualise our inner world as a planet. Planets don't only orbit around the Sun, their own gravitational pull influences other planets too, much like the Moon influences our tides. Each of us lives in our own unique planet that has been constructed from birth. It contains a specific atmosphere, culture, language, with many countries, cities, and neighbourhoods. Each of those has specific names. For example, there may be a country called "Childhood". In that country, there are cities that are made of good memories and other cities made of unpleasant memories. Within those cities, there are specific neighbourhoods that have stories such as "The Day My Mother Shamed Me" or "Laughing With My Sister". There are other countries too, like "Marriage", "Sex", "Work", and "Adolescence". Some people have so many stories around a theme; for example, anger may be a theme that can grow into a city, or even a country.

With this conceptualisation, we can become aware of where we are in our world when we are in the presence of other people in our relationships. Amy started a conversation with her partner Samantha from the country called "Adult Love", in the City of "Comfort", and in the neighbourhood of "When I feel loved". In that moment, Amy poured much comfort, love, and relaxing energy into the in-between relationship space. She felt strongly connected with Samantha. The relationship felt lovely in that moment. Then, Samantha suggested baking together. For Amy, the neighbourhood of "Baking" doesn't belong in the city of "Comfort", it is part of her neighbourhood called "When I'm Shouted At", in the country called "I'm Worthless". It is connected to a painful memory of baking with her mother, who was in a hurry and shouted at Amy inappropriately for making a mess. In that moment, the mere mention of baking yanked Amy away from the country of "Adult Love" straight into "I'm Worthless", and she responded to Samantha's suggestion from that part of her world: her body language moved away from Samantha, her tone of voice changed, and she abruptly refused the suggestion. Suddenly, the in-between relationship space turned from sunny to stormy. Samantha felt bad because she wondered if she had said something wrong. Samantha wasn't aware of Amy's childhood memory and was flabbergasted by such a sudden change in mood.

When we are aware of our world and all of its countries, cities, and neighbourhoods, we can inform our partner(s) where we are so that communication can be adjusted accordingly. For example, Amy might have said: "the idea of baking together is not a good thought for me and I'm now feeling upset because I remember an awful memory of my childhood." If Amy had communicated that, it would have given a clue for Samantha to know where she was and would have made better sense of the change in the relationship temperature.

We need to spend some time looking after our world. Sometimes we can prioritise the relationship but sometimes we need to prioritise ourselves. If there is a particular city that is in ruins and feeling very painful because of past trauma, it is important to attend to it. Equally, our world never stops evolving because new neighbourhoods form every time we have new experiences, so it is important to keep getting to know our own world. With good communication, we can also get to know some of our partners' world, and we can develop an awareness of their particular sensitive neighbourhoods and adapt how we speak so that we can make sure there is a common language.

A popular theory by Hendrix (2001) and LaKelly Hunt and Hendrix (2013) asserts that we choose our partner(s) with a subconscious filter of looking for traits that our parents have, and we are trying to resolve the "unfinished business" of our childhood through the adult relationship with our partner(s). Although this theory can be very helpful for some people, and it is often confirmed when observing the struggles that some couples have, it can also be misunderstood as some people do not resonate with this.

If a partner reminds us of a trait our parents have, or if we are in a relationship situation that feels like one that happened in childhood, it may simply be considered as an opportunity to attend to our own world, rather than believing that we subconsciously made it happen. Human relationships are so complex that I prefer not to discount any theories; the more we have, the better!

If we don't pay attention to our own world, or if we ignore our partner(s)'s, or, worse, dismiss their world because we think our world is better, we can make the in-between relationship an unpleasant space to be. If the people in the relationship don't invest in the relationship and feed it on a regular basis with love, care, commitment, tenderness, laughter, companionship, support, and attention, then the relationship slowly erodes and eventually dies.

LOVE

We can't talk about intimate relationships without talking about love. It seems that love is one of the most mysterious human emotions. Love is a grand word. It can be vague too. It can have multiple meanings depending on the context, culture, or event. Love can be a powerful word. But it can also be meaningless or even dangerous when used inappropriately, for example "I beat you up for your own good, because I love you".

Love is an enormous driver to our life force, our motivations, our desire to be in relationships, our search for meaning. Love is the main theme of all our most poignant human stories; we see it everywhere, in religious texts like the Bible, Greek tragedies, Shakespeare plays, all the way to our modern stories and blockbuster films. Whether the story is about betrayal, vengeance, murder, war, or comedy, the common thread is love, the search for it, the acquisition of it, or the loss of it.

People who struggle in their intimate relationships often say "all I want is to be loved", or "I feel very unloved". But do we even know what we mean by that? What is the actual search? Would we know if we felt it? How would we know? What is love supposed to feel like? In our society, we often hear "all we need is love", "as long as there is love, the rest will fall into place". But is it true? Is it really all we need?

If we can't properly define love, it is not a surprise that many people might feel unhappy in their relationships because they think there isn't enough love. One way that we can understand love better is by accepting that love isn't just one emotion. Love can take multiple shapes and be associated with multiple feelings. What if there were many types of love? Perhaps we feel unhappy because we've been fixated on one type of love, not realising that our lives might be filled with love, but of a different type.

The seven types of Greek love

To elucidate the mystery of love, the Ancient Greeks deconstructed it into seven types (Barker, 2018b).

Eros is sexual love and erotic passion. This is the closest version of our modern understanding of romantic love as narrated in stories; the feeling of love combined with sexual satisfaction.

Philia is the love we have for friends. It is a love of loyalty and commitment. It describes intimacy that is non-sexual yet extremely potent.

Storge is familial love, the love for people who are family and feel like family. For example, it can describe the love parents have for their children. But it can also be the love that we have for our long-term intimate partner(s) because those relationships can feel family-like and less passionately erotic. Yet, when people feel Storge love, it is still a powerful type of love, that many people can dismiss because of the absence of Eros.

Agape is universal love, the love for humanity (including strangers), the love for nature or the love for God. Agape can be described as charity love, the selfless altruism that we have for the welfare of others. I would like to think that Agape can be the love that therapists have for their clients because I do believe that therapy is love (a non-sexual, non-familial, yet potent altruistic love).

Ludus is the playful or uncommitted kind of love. It can be teasing, dancing, flirting, or seducing. The focus is on fun with no strings attached. Many people dismiss casual sexual encounters as unimportant, but, in fact, many can have a strong temporary connection of this type of love. Although Ludus is uncomplicated and undemanding, it might be a part of long-term intimate relationships, especially those who thrive in Relationship Anarchy. Ludus is not the same as Eros, but more compatible with Philia.

Pragma is love focused on pragmatism. It is the love concerned with long-term interests and goals in a practical sense. Personal qualities, compatibilities, shared goals, and vision for the future are prioritised over sexual attraction. Many relationships start off with Eros and/or Ludus and, over time, transform into different versions of Storge and/or Pragma. This is not bad or wrong, it is the natural progression of many intimate relationships. It is important to note that Pragma is a type of love that is as valid and important as the other types, even if it is not recognised by our modern society as such.

Philautia is self-love, self-care, and self-compassion. A lot of people find it uncomfortable to talk about because they fear that others will criticise them for being arrogant or a narcissist. Of course, an excessive amount of self-love at the expense of other people's well-being is not good. However, most people could do with a little bit more Philautia. Having a good amount of self-love means that we can appraise properly our own worth as we stand in the world, how we interact with others, how we put the right boundaries in for ourselves, and how we care for ourselves when we need to, from deciding to take a break when life is too hard, to celebrating our own success. As a clinical sexologist, I would like to add that masturbation is Philautia too because it is a wonderful activity of self-care and a good quality time for loving ourselves.

I think the idea of the seven types of Greek love is useful because it can offer a different perspective on our sense of loving and being loved in our intimate relationship(s). For example, the waning of Eros doesn't necessarily spell catastrophe if there is an awareness that it is morphing into a different type of love that is just as important and valid. Sometimes, when we think that our relationship isn't loving, it might mean we are not recognising the type of love that exists in the relationship. This is not to say that we have to be looking for evidence of love when there is none. Some relationships do definitely develop into an absence of love, where there is not enough gravitational pull any longer because each planet has drifted too far away from each other, and eventually the Sun dims and the star dies. When that happens, it is best to exit the planetary system and find a new one, indeed.

THE 5 LOVE LANGUAGES®

Gary Chapman (2015) developed his theory of the 5 Love Languages® to help us understand better how we give and receive love. According to Chapman, we tend to express love in five different ways, and, similarly, we perceive being loved differently too. The 5 Love Languages® are:

Physical Touch: when someone expresses their love mostly through touching their partner(s) like hugs, caresses, or just simply holding hands. Some people feel most loved when they are being touched in some of those ways too.

Gift Giving: when someone expresses their love with objects. It doesn't have to be expensive gifts, they can be small things, but it is their way to say "I love you". Some people feel loved primarily when they receive objects from their partners. Often, if the gifts are thoughtful, they have a much bigger impact. It can be flowers, a take-away meal, or even a post-it with a loving message on it.

Quality Time: when someone expresses their love primarily by spending time with their partner(s). The quality time doesn't have to involve doing something amazing; it could be watching television together, playing a game, or having dinner together talking with no phones around. Some people feel most loved when their partner takes time to clear their schedule to be with them.

Words of Affirmation: when someone expresses their love by verbalising compliments to them such as "you look good in this dress", "you are a good cook", "you have a good sense of humour", or by affirming their love such as "I love you", "I love being with you", "It's so good to be together". Equally, the people whose love language is words of affirmation feel most loved when they hear their partner(s) say those things. Some people need verbal affirmations about looking good, others prefer comments to be about their personality, and some prefer hearing how good they are at doing things.

Acts of Service: when someone expresses their love by doing things for their partner(s) or for the household, if they live together. For example, it may be cooking, doing the housework, or doing DIY. Some people feel most loved when they see their partners doing things for them.

I love Chapman's idea of the 5 Love Languages® because it makes it easy to understand how miscommunication about love can happen.

1. Patrick is annoyed that Peter seems to never have time for him. Each time Patrick asks Peter to sit down with him and relax (Quality Time), Peter keeps saying that he's busy with chores: sweeping the leaves in the garden, hoovering the carpet, cleaning the windows, and on and on and on (Acts of Service). Patrick thinks that Peter is avoiding him because he doesn't really love him. The truth is that Peter shows Patrick love every day with his own Love Language that Patrick doesn't recognise. Equally, Peter doesn't hear Patrick's bid for love when he asks him to sit with him and, therefore, dismisses it.

2. Rachel believes that Matt doesn't really love or fancy her because he never says that she's pretty or sexy (Words of Affirmation). Instead, he surprises her with numerous small gifts every week (Gift Giving). The objects don't mean anything to Rachel and she feels starved of love. She doesn't understand that Matt is actually saying "I love you" without words but with gifts. Matt feels disappointed because he doesn't understand why Rachel isn't beaming at his thoughtful gifts. He doesn't realise that it is not what Rachel understands as a communication of love.

When people understand each other's Love Language, they can adapt their love communication by using their partner's Love Language for the best effect. For example, Peter became more attentive when Patrick asked him to relax with him and decided to stop doing chores to show Patrick his love the way he needs it. Similarly, Patrick was happier to see Peter doing the housework because he then understood it was his version of saying "I love you".

Matt paid more attention to giving a gift to Rachel accompanied with words like "I bought this for you to say that I love you and you're an amazing person", which worked better for Rachel. She started to give him gifts to show her love for him because she understood that objects were also the way he felt loved the most.

THE SCIENCE OF LOVE

Love is not one emotion. It is a complex experience that happens within diverse relationships, with people of all sexual orientations, all genders, all racial diversities and all cultures. Love has been observed objectively by science in studying our brain, which means that although love is highly subjective and is felt differently by each of us, it is also a universal experience because it is essential for our survival. Machin (2022) writes:

> being with a supportive social network reduced the risk of mortality by 50 per cent. That places it on a par with quitting smoking, and of more influence than maintaining a healthy BMI measure.
> (2022, p.23)

There are four key neurochemicals underpinning our experiences of love that are involved in our brain when we first meet someone we like, and also when we interact with our loved ones in long-term relationships. These neurochemicals are involved in *all* forms of human love, whether it is interacting with a romantic partner, a friend, a family member, and so on. But, here, we will mainly focus on romantic love.

> *Oxytocin:* is an important neurochemical at the start of relationships because it lowers our inhibitions and it has a calming effect on the "fear centre" of our brain (the Amygdala). Oxytocin makes it easier to meet people we don't know and form relationships with them. Oxytocin is released with Dopamine.
> *Dopamine:* is the reward chemical (among other functions), making us feel good when we do something we enjoy.
> Oxytocin and Dopamine are in partnership at the beginning of a relationship to help us focus on the new person we're dating

by making our brain more open to new experiences. When we meet a new person, we have to learn a lot of new information about them and we need to have the new information stored in our long-term memory so that we can retrieve it when we meet them again (it is helpful to maximise the success of the next meeting by preparing ourselves based on what we have learnt about the person). Oxytocin and Dopamine are also a good partnership for giving us the motivation to build the new relationship. While Oxytocin makes us more relaxed when we meet a new person, Dopamine gives us the vigour to motivate behaviours that will promote building bonds.

Serotonin: while Oxytocin and Dopamine levels go up when we meet someone new, it appears our Serotonin goes down. Scientists are still trying to figure out why. The most accepted hypothesis is that low Serotonin is associated with obsessive behaviours and therefore having less Serotonin makes us slightly "obsessed" with the new person, which gives us even more motivation to carry on seeing them, co-ordinate our diary with them, make us care about what they feel and what they think of us. Oxytocin is a lovely and wonderful neurochemical when we start a relationship and it is particularly potent when we have sex (with short-term and long-term partners) and in childbirth. But it is not so potent in helping us maintain long-term romantic relationships. This is when the fourth neurochemical of love comes in handy.

Beta-Endorphin: underpins the love in all human long-term relationships (including friendships). It is our body's natural opiate, but Beta-Endorphin also plays a powerful part in our social life. Whenever we interact with someone we're in a relationship with, we get a hit of Beta-Endorphin, it makes us feel happy and joyous. It is the neurochemical that makes us miss our loved ones when we're apart, and it is what motivates us to return to them. Beta-Endorphin is not only released when we have sex, it is released in all pleasant human interactions with our romantic partners, friends, people: laughing together, talking with each other, singing together, dancing together, doing exercise together. It is released in one-to-one connections and in crowds too: watching or participating in a sporting event, attending a concert, having a party, and so on.

In the context of romantic love, when we first "fall in love", and we get the lovely cocktails of Oxytocin (calm), Dopamine (vigour), low Serotonin (slightly obsessed) and Beta-Endorphin (joy), another part of our brain switches off. It is the part that is involved with our ability to have intuition ("gut feeling") that help us perceive the intention of a person. So, we can be "blind" to the true personality of that person we're falling in love with. It appears that the common phrase "love is blind" is actually scientific. While we might think that the person we're falling in love with is really wonderful, our friends might have the "gut feeling" that this person isn't really all that good for us.

When we first "fall in love" with someone, the feeling of love happens in the subconscious and emotional part of our brain, deep in the ancient region attached to the Limbic System, in the part called Nucleus Accumbens (there is a lot of Dopamine and Oxytocin receptors in that part of the brain). In the following few weeks of dating someone and getting to know them, the feeling of love moves from the Nucleus Accumbens to the Caudate Head (still in the Limbic System). The Caudate Head has many connections with the Cortex part of our brain (the modern part involved in social skills, empathy, trust, and reciprocity). So, in the dating stage, we experience the feeling of love on a subconscious and deeply emotional level (passion and lust) and on a conscious level at the same time (empathy and trust). As the romantic relationship develops, more and more of the Pre-frontal Cortex is engaged in the experience of love. The Pre-frontal Cortex is involved in rational thinking, so this is when passion and lust transforms into planning for the future, consciously co-ordinating life with our partner(s), further building trust, empathy, reciprocity, and compassion. This explains why Eros can become Pragma.

When we deeply bond with someone, we can observe what scientists call "Biobehavioural synchrony": people who are bonded mirror each other behaviourally and physiological: heart rate, blood pressure, and body temperature become in synchrony too. Machin (2022) observes:

> it is this eye contact – combined with the degree of synchrony in non-verbal behaviour – that has the biggest impact on the extent of neural synchrony; the extent of conversation is not a factor. This distinction perhaps indicate the evolutionarily ancient nature

of biobehavioural synchrony but also its lifelong applicability to the maintenance of our closest bonds, for it enables the most profound attachments to develop from the moment we emerge as pre-verbal infants.

(2022, p. 82)

It seems that nature has created some powerful organic mechanisms to make our brain (emotional and rational parts), our physiology, and our psychology impressively focused in human beings starting and maintaining relationships. This may be because love is not just a lovely feeling we have when we're in a good relationship, love is an integral part of our survival.

THE RULE FOR GOOD ROMANTIC RELATIONSHIPS IS … THERE IS NO RULE

Throughout this book, I have explained how much diversity there is in being human and there aren't fixed rules (or dogma) that can be followed to ensure happiness because we are all so different. The very basis of psychotherapy and clinical sexology is to help people find their own wisdom. Indeed, when people seek help, they often fear that they're broken, but they are not. They are simply lost and confused and find it difficult to access their own wisdom for their own path of emotional regulation, problem resolutions, and well-being. Although psychotherapy and clinical sexology offer much evidence-based scientific information to guide and support people, each will ultimately have to walk their own path. Sadly, some of the confusion that can maintain people's distress are the very "rules" attempting to help people that are so prevalent on social media and blogs. When it comes to romantic relationships, there are many myths, just as many as there are sex myths. Be mindful of some of those "experts" mostly because their advice might not apply to everyone. If they don't sound right to us, we need to ignore them; we are a better expert on our own life experience than any experts who don't know us!

Let me break down some common myths about relationships:

1. You don't have to have your life "sorted" before you can date successfully. Many people have issues with their housing, work, health, finances, or unhelpful habits, and yet are still able to date

and even find a wonderful life partner(s). In fact, it is sometimes when faced with adversities that we can find the right person (or people) for us. Remember, love is an integral part of our survival.

2. You can start dating as soon as you have broken up with your ex. There isn't any recommended period of time of "being by yourself to heal". Dating after a break-up isn't necessarily a "rebound". For some, it might be good to spend some time to heal before meeting new people, but not for others. It is not a rule.

3. Unconditional love is only appropriate from a parent to their under-aged children. When people become adults, there are conditions to love, for example the condition of respect, trust, and boundaries. If someone manipulates someone else, betrays them, or abuses them physically, psychologically, or financially, there is no entitlement or automatic right to love or be loved. In most instances, love needs to be conditional in order to thrive.

4. A long-term relationship is not a sign of a successful relationship. Someone feeling bad in a relationship because their partner abused them emotionally for many years is worse than a relationship that lasted six months where the people in it had a lot of fun and decided to call it quits for one reason or another.

5. Ending a relationship is not the worst that can ever happen. In many cases, it is the best that people can do to look after themselves and those around them. I often hear couples staying with each other "for the sake of the children". This is misguided because children do suffer when they live with two adults who dislike and resent each other. Children are very good at feeling the atmosphere of the relationship that their parents co-create.

When we think about how we select people to date, we tend to look for the positive factors: what we want and like in people. But what about the negative factors contributing to who we choose to date? Csajbók and Berkics (2022) conducted an interesting study that looked at the undesirable characteristics that are important for people in their mate choice. They found that there are seven "dealbreakers":

Hostile (unfriendly, moody)
Unattractive (physically)
Unambitious (no sense of purpose or direction in life)

Filthy (poor hygiene)
Arrogant (egotistical)
Clingy (wanting to commit too soon)
Abusive (aggressive)

The study suggests that people tend to prefer to look at the "deal-makers" (the desirable factors we like in people) rather than the "dealbreakers". This is perhaps due to the neurochemicals of love and our survival instinct of needing to be with people.

THE THIRD ELEMENT

Barker and Gabb (2016) conducted an extensive survey of people in relationships. They found that the people who were more satisfied with their relationships were the ones who identified their partner or themselves as the "most important person", not the ones who saw their children as the most important people. I'm sure it is quite challenging for parents to read this but, in fact, it makes sense. Children live within the relational space that is co-created by the parents. If the relational space is solid, the children tend to be happier. If the relational space is unbalanced, because the adults in the relationship feel neglected or unsupported, the children will feel the tension in that space. It can be an emotional and moral challenge for parents to re-frame their "most important person" as their partner again, but it might be the best for everybody. However, this is not all. Barker and Gabb (2016) also find that relationships are more stable when there is a "third element", like the third leg of a stool, to stabilise the relationship.

> For parents, the third element is often their children. For some people pets are crucial. For others, religion is the vital third element. For some it's their interests or hobbies. For many people the crucial third element is their friends. For some people in non-monogamous relationships, it's their other partners.
>
> (2016, pp. 139–140)

THE GOOD RELATIONSHIP CHECKLIST

There is no rule-fits-all. Yet, being in a relationship requires knowledge and skills. So, here, I am offering the relationship checklist that

I came up with, based on my experience of working with many intimate relationships.

1. *Love:* have a common understanding of each person's different love language. It can be love expressions done verbally or non-verbally. They can be the small, everyday acts of love rather than big gestures. It is fostering a sense that they are their partner's most important person, choosing to be with them every day. It may include having intimate conversations with each other, and fun activities like dancing together or exercising together for that Beta-Endorphin hit.

2. *Sex:* the people in the intimate relationship need to be clear about their desires, needs, wants, turn-ons, ideas, values, and visions about their sex life to foster an ongoing erotic conversation so that all people fully consent to it. It includes the expression of not wanting sex.

3. *Appreciation:* paying attention to expressing what you appreciate about your partner(s) being in your life. It is an important way to invest in the relationship, and nurture it so that it keeps strong enough to withstand inevitable future turbulence.

4. *Visiting Planets:* it is a good idea to share with your partner(s) what your own planet is made of; what are the important big countries, cities, and neighbourhoods. A deeper understanding of each partner's world increases intimacy and creates a map of their unique planetary system in order to navigate it better.

5. *Respect and Boundaries:* when choosing to be in a relationship, we need to make a commitment to support our partner(s) emotionally and practically. Respecting our partner(s) is to accept their qualities and their flaws. We can't cherry-pick, we have to accept the full package, without attempting to change them. We have to be tolerant of them and their mistakes, or their difference in opinions. In return, we can expect the same respect. Boundaries are explicitly knowing what is OK and what is not OK in our relationship. There are some universal unacceptable behaviours such as being abusive. But there are other boundaries that may need to be defined and agreed upon explicitly by all people involved in the intimate relationship. Respect and boundaries help with recruiting your partner(s) as a team member.

SUMMARY

Whether we are introverts or extroverts, we all have one thing in common as human beings: we are relationship people, we thrive in connections, and love is an integral part of our survival. For introverted people, the interactions with others may be draining and have to be paced out with plenty of "alone time" in between, whereas the extroverted people seek proximity with others to recharge their batteries. Some of us prefer connections with animals or the communion with nature. One thing is certain, human beings don't survive without connections.

We have many different ways to be in relationships with others: friendships, student-teacher, parent-child, casual lovers, monogamous/non-monogamous intimate relationships, and so on. All of them are important. But when it comes to intimate relationships and love, it is easy to be confused and to find it difficult to understand how to find good partner(s) who will love us the way we want and need them to. There is poor sex education and there is poor relationship education, so we rely on what we can grasp from social media, blogs, or "experts" prescribing a formula-that-fits-all, which can actually be unhelpful.

The best way to find and nurture intimate relationships is to know your own planet well, get to know your partner(s)' planet and co-create your planetary system based on full informed consent, respect and boundaries, with the knowledge that as we age, we change, and as we change, the system changes. We have to be flexible enough to adapt and reconfigure the system as we go along, and embrace the different types of love we might feel.

Reflective questions:

1 What are the important relationships in your life, including friendships, work-related relationships, intimate relationships?

2 What are the relationships you have dismissed as unimportant but realised they were actually worthy of nurturing after reading this chapter?

3 What are your thoughts and feelings about all the different ways people can be in intimate relationships?

4 Reflecting on your own intimate relationships, past and present, do you think that you have had explicit conversations about monogamy/non-monogamy before committing to them?

5 Reflecting on your ideas about love, past and present, what do you think has influenced you the most in assessing whether you were loved or not? Have you mistaken a different type of love for an absence of love?

6 What might be considerations that you haven't thought of before about navigating the development of your relationships, moving from one type of love to another?

7 What is your main love language? What is the main love language of your partner(s)?

8 What might you do differently now that you know your love language and the one of your partner(s)?

9 Reflecting on the good relationship checklist, what are the items you need to think more about?

10 What has been most surprising for you about this chapter?

FURTHER READING

The 5 Love Languages®. The Secret to Love That Lasts, by Gary Chapman. (2015).

The Course of Love, by Alain de Botton. (2016).

Rewriting The Rules. An Anti Self-Help Guide to Love, Sex and Relationships, by Meg-John Barker. (2018).

REFERENCES

Barker, M.J. (2018a). *The Psychology of Sex*. Routledge. Abingdon, Oxon.

Barker, M.J. (2018b). *Rewriting the Rules. An Anti Self-Help Guide to Love, Sex and Relationships*. Second Ed. Routledge. Abingdon. Oxon.

Barker, M.J., & Gabb, J. (2016). *The Secrets of Enduring Love. How to Make Relationship Last.* Vermilion. London.

Bowlby, J. (1969). *Attachment. Attachment and Loss, Volume 1.* Pimlico. London.

Bowlby, J. (1973). *Seperation. Anxiety and Anger. Attachment and Loss, Volume 2.* Pimlico. London.

Bowlby, J. (1980). *Loss. Sadness and Depression. Attachment and Loss, Volume 3.* Pimlico. London.

Chapman, G. D. (2015). *The 5 Love Languages®: The Secret to Love That Lasts.* Northfield Publishing. Chicago.

Csajbók, Z., & Berkics, M. (2022). Seven Deadly Sins of Potential Romantic Partners: The Dealbreakers of Mate Choice. *Personality and Individual Differences*, 186, 111334.

Fern, J. (2020). *Polysecure. Attachment, Trauma and Consensual Nonmonogamy.* Thorntree Press, LLC. Portland, OR.

Hendrix, H. (2001). *Getting the Love You Want. A Guide for Couples.* Simon & Schuster UK Ltd. London.

LaKelly Hunt and Hendrix (2013). *Making Marriage Simple. 10 Truths for Changing the Relationship You Have into the One You Want.* Piatkus. London.

Machin, A. (2022). *Why We Love.* The Orion Publishing Group Ltd. London.

Perel, E. (2006). *Mating In Captivity. Unlocking Erotic Intelligence.* HarperCollins. New York.

Savage, D. (2005). *The Commitment.* Plume. Penguin Group. London.

Schnarch, D. (2009). *Passionate Marriage. Keeping Love & Intimacy Alive in Committed Relationships.* W.W. Norton & Company, Inc. New York.

Stewart, I., & Joines, V. (1987). *TA Today. A New Introduction to Transactional Analysis.* Lifespace Publishing. Nottingham, England.

SEXUAL OFFENDING

I have so far discussed human sexuality in an inclusive way to normalise the large diversities of sexual and relational expressions, bust-
ing some myths, and offering a sex-positive lens to thinking about
gender, sex, and relationships.

However, it doesn't mean that all sexual expressions need to be
embraced. Indeed, there are some clear sexual behaviours that are an
offence by law, such as rape and coercing a child into sexual activities, because these have tremendously damaging psychological and
physical impacts on victims.

There is much conflation of "healthy" and "unhealthy" sexual
behaviours in mainstream society. Many sexual behaviours deemed
as "unhealthy" are in fact normal, even if unusual, as I explained in
Chapter 6. I have previously discussed that there is no normal in
sexology, so how can we define what is outside of normal if there is
no normal? Rather than using a "normal" framework, perhaps it is
more useful to use an "offence" one. But even that is not so simple,
because, in some countries and cultures, it is an offence to have sex
with people of the same gender.

So, can we say that when a sexual behaviour becomes an offence
(harming others), then it stops being "normal"? Some consider "not
normal" to mean "counter-nature" such as paedophilia, but, as I will
explain in this chapter, some paedophiles do not offend.

Since the concepts of normal, natural and offence are culturally
constructed and have varying laws to reflect that culture, we can see
that these topics are not so straightforward. For example, in the UK,
it is abhorrent, offensive, and illegal to have sex with a child, but in

DOI: 10.4324/9781003276913-10

some countries it is common practice to marry a 13-year-old girl to an older man.

It is also important to remember that there is a difference between fantasies and behaviours. Some sexual behaviours are offending acts, harm others, and are illegal. Fantasies are not. Some people say that fantasising about any type of sexual offence is a gateway to acting it out. Perhaps it is, for some people, but for many it is not.

SEXUAL OFFENDING BEHAVIOURS

Here are some of the sexual practices that are deemed unnatural, illegal, and offensive in the UK:

Bestiality is the act of sexually penetrating a living animal vaginally or anally by humans on animals or animals on humans. In England and Wales, penetrative sex between a human and a living animal is a sexual offence under the Sexual Offence Act 2003. Sexual activity other than penetration could be an offence related to cruelty to animals. The fifth edition of the Diagnostic and Statistical Manual of Mental Disorders by the American Psychiatric Association (APA, DSM-5, 2013) uses the term "zoophilia", which is categorised under "Other Specified Paraphilic Disorder", which means that it doesn't fully meet all the criteria for paraphilic disorders but nevertheless "cause clinically significant distress or impairment in social, occupational, or other important areas of functioning" (APA, 2013, p. 705). It is worth mentioning here that bestiality is not related to furries mentioned in Chapter 6 (those who enjoy having sex wearing animal costumes) because these specific sexual practices are done between consenting human adults.

Non-consensual rubbing, also called "frottage" or "frotteurism", is mostly practised when people are in a crowded confined space, for example, the London Underground at rush hour, when the offending person will rub against someone else for their sexual pleasure, without consent. It is considered to be a sexual assault under the Sexual Offences Act, 2003, however the term "frottage" or "frotteurism" isn't directly mentioned in the Sexual Offences Act. The DSM-5 defines "Frotteuristic Disorder" as "recurrent and intense sexual arousal from touching or rubbing against a nonconsenting person, as manifested by fantasies, urges, or behaviors" and "the individual has acted on these sexual urges with a nonconsenting person, or the sexual urges or fantasies cause clinically significant distress or impairment in social, occupational, or other important areas of functioning" for a period of six months at least (APA, 2013, p. 691).

Upskirting is the offending practice of using a device (mirror or phone with extension equipment) to look under someone's skirt (or dress) without their consent. When done with phones, it has become more common that the offending person would film or take pictures. This is obviously a practice that is commonly done by men to women, but as there is an increasing number of people with penises feeling more comfortable wearing skirts and dresses, they could become a new population exposed to the risk of upskirting. It is an offence under the Voyeurism Offences Act 2019.

Incest describes sexual contact between close family-related people such as siblings, parents and their children, grandparents and their grandchildren, uncles/aunts with their nephews or cousins, or foster parents. The legal definition of incest (Sexual Offences Act 1956) states that if it involves a child, step-relationships are included under the Sexual Offences Act, 2003. Some people who are in a group of close friendships having sex with each other may be described as "incestuous", but it is not so by the proper sense of the term. What is considered incest may vary from country to country. For example, it is perceived as OK to have sexual relationships with cousins in some countries, but incest is illegal in England and Wales under the Sexual Offences Act, 2003.

Necrophilia describes sexual intercourse or sexual attraction to corpses. The DSM-5 categorised necrophilia under "Other Specified Paraphilic Disorder" (APA, 2013, p. 705). It is thought to be a rare disorder. Some people enjoy the fantasy of having sex with a dead person and some may incorporate it in role plays occasionally, when one partner pretends to be dead or lifeless while their sexual partner touches them. If it is a genuine role play and fully consented to, it is not a disorder nor an offence, and it should not be described as necrophilia. In England and Wales (Sexual Offences Act 2003, section 70), the actual sexual penetration of a corpse is a sexual offence and punishable by law.

Paedophilia. First, I would like to briefly clarify some terminology to position paedophilia:

Paedophilia: primary attraction to pre-pubescent children.

Hebephilia: primary attraction to pubescent children.

Teleiophilia: primary attraction to adults.

Gerontophilia: primary attraction to the elderly.

Paedophilia is considered a mental health disorder by the DSM-5 under "paedophilic disorder", which criteria include: "recurrent, intense sexually arousing fantasies, sexual urges, or behaviors involving sexual activity with a prepubescent child or children (generally aged 13 years or younger)" and "the individual has acted on these sexual urges, or the sexual urges or fantasies cause marked distress or interpersonal difficulty" and "the individual is at least 16 years and at least 5 years older than the child or children". These diagnostic criteria also stipulate that the disorder does not include "an individual in late adolescence involved in an ongoing sexual relationship with a 12- or 13-year old" (APA, 2013, p. 697).

It is illegal to have sexual activities with a child, including showing explicit sexual images, exposing a child to watch a sexual act, or sexually touching a child under the Sexual Offences Act, 2003.

Dr Cantor (n.d.), one of the few specialist clinicians in paedophilia, offers his insight on his website that: (1) paedophilic brain processing does not differ from non-paedophilic brain processing, (2) the paedophilic brain structure is slightly different from the typical brain, (3) the brain of paedophiles "lights up" in the same pattern as non-paedophiles, however paedophiles respond to stimuli of children rather than adults. This may indicate an uncomfortable hypothesis that paedophiles are not so different from non-paedophile people, and perhaps it is akin to a sexual orientation.

Sarah D. Goode (2010) defines paedophilia as a sexual orientation too:

Paedophilia, as we currently understand it, is the medical diagnosis of a fixed sexual orientation which may or may not manifest itself in actual behaviour towards a child.

(2010, p. 10)

Through her research, Goode came to three main conclusions: (1) as uncomfortable as it makes us feel, paedophiles exist; (2) the media and policies that demonise paedophiles make the situation worse; (3) the current criminal-justice interventions do not work. She adds:

> The lack of help for adults sexually attracted to children is further exacerbated by the lack of knowledge about this area. There is a reluctance to support research to learn more about the experiences of paedophiles or the incidence of sexual attraction to children in the general adult population. Until policy-makers and others find the courage to endorse and commission research in this area, and disseminate relevant findings, child protection agencies are operating with one hand tied behind their backs.
>
> (2010, p. 169)

Violent Practices (Extreme) include becoming sexually aroused by seriously harming another person such as maiming, murder, or rape. Extreme violent practices are behaviours that reflect underlying psychological disorders and they are considered anti-social and criminal behaviours, of course. Fantasising about raping or being raped is quite common and does not imply an actual desire to rape or be raped. However, for some people, the boundaries between rough sex and consent to serious harm can be confusing. The UK government (2022) updated their policy on Domestic Violence to clarify its position regarding consent to serious harm for sexual gratification:

The Act makes clear, in England and Wales, that:

- a person is unable to consent to the infliction of harm that results in actual bodily harm or other more serious injury or, by extension, to their own death, for the purposes of obtaining sexual gratification.
- a defendant is unable to rely on a victim's consent to the infliction of such harm as part of any so-called "rough sex gone wrong" defence.
- an exception remains, in relation to the transmission of sexually transmitted infections (STIs) where, in certain circumstances, a person may consent to the risk of acquiring an STI. This exception is in line with current case law.

• the law applies in all situations and is not limited to those which might also amount to incidents of domestic abuse.

Non-consensual voyeurism or exposure is different from the legal and consensual practice of voyeurism and exhibitionism described in Chapter 6. The Sexual Offences Act, 2003 identify exposure as intentionally exposing genitals and the intention that someone will see them and be caused alarm or distress.

The Sexual Offences Act, 2003 regarding voyeurism states (Section 67):

(1) A person commits an offence if–
   (a) for the purpose of obtaining sexual gratification, he observes another person doing a private act, and
   (b) he knows that the other person does not consent to being observed for his sexual gratification.
(2) A person commits an offence if–
   (a) he operates equipment with the intention of enabling another person to observe, for the purpose of obtaining sexual gratification, a third person (B) doing a private act, and
   (b) he knows that B does not consent to his operating equipment with that intention.
(3) A person commits an offence if–
   (a) he records another person (B) doing a private act,
   (b) he does so with the intention that he or a third person will, for the purpose of obtaining sexual gratification, look at an image of B doing the act, and
   (c) he knows that B does not consent to his recording the act with that intention.
(4) A person commits an offence if he instals equipment, or constructs or adapts a structure or part of a structure, with the intention of enabling himself or another person to commit an offence under subsection (1).

The DSM-5 classifies "Voyeuristic Disorder" if an adult (at least 18 years of age) has a "recurrent and intense sexual arousal from observing an unsuspecting person who is naked, in the process of disrobing, or engaging in sexual activity, as manifested by fantasies, urges, or behaviors" and the individual has "acted on these sexual urges with a nonconsenting person, or the sexual urges or fantasies cause clinically significant distress or impairment in social, occupational, or other important areas of functioning" over a period of six months at least (APA, 2013, p. 686). The diagnostic criteria for "Exhibitionistic Disorder" are a "recurrent and intense sexual arousal from the exposure of one's genitals to an unsuspecting person, as manifested by fantasies, urges or behaviors" and the individual "has acted on these sexual urges with a nonconsenting person, or the sexual urges or fantasies cause clinically significant distress or impairment in social, occupational, or other important areas of functioning" over a period of 6 months at least (APA, 2013, p. 689). Non-consensual voyeurism and exposure are punishable by law in England and Wales under the Sexual Offences Act, 2003.

Extreme BDSM/Kink practices – this is a contentious one because there is an argument between what the law considers harm and what some extreme BDSMers think as consensual. This particularly refers to BDSM activities that involve cutting, drawing blood, or leaving significant marks that take time to heal, which, in law, could be deemed to be actual bodily harm. The DSM-5 classifies some BDSM and kink behaviours as mental health disorders:

(1) "Sexual Masochism Disorder", the diagnostic criteria are: "recurrent and intense sexual arousal from the act of being humiliated, beaten, bound, or otherwise made to suffer, as manifested by fantasies, urges, or behaviors" and "the fantasies, sexual urges, or behaviours cause clinically significant distress or impairment in social, occupational, or other important areas of functioning" over a period of 6 months at least (APA, 2013, p. 694).

(2) "Sexual Sadism Disorder" is "recurrent and intense sexual arousal from physical or psychological suffering of another person, as manifested by fantasies, urges, or behaviors" and "the individual has acted on these sexual urges with a nonconsenting person, or the sexual urges or fantasies cause clinically significant distress or impairment in social, occupational, or other important areas of functioning" over a period of six months of more (APA, 2013, p. 695).

(3) "Fetishistic Disorder" is "over a period of at least 6 months, recurrent and intense sexual arousal from either the use of non-living objects or a highly specific focus on nongenital body part(s), as manifested by fantasies, urges, or behaviors" and "the

fantasies, sexual urges, or behaviors cause clinically significant distress or impairment in social, occupational, or other important areas of functioning" and "the fetish objects are not limited to articles of clothing used in cross-dressing (as in transvestic disorder) or devices specifically designed for the purpose of tactile genital stimulation (e.g. vibrator)" (APA, 2013, p. 700).

As you can see, these diagnostic criteria, as with all paraphilic disorders, have to include the presence of significant distress or impairment in the important areas of life functioning. Clinicians cannot formulate a disorder diagnosis only with "unusual" sexual behaviours.

Shahbaz and Chirinos (2017) offer a helpful ethical guide to distinguish "healthy" and "unhealthy" BDSM behaviours, aimed at therapists working with kink and BDSM, which include: consent, the vision and philosophy of their BDSM practice, and how their values align with their practises.

ILLEGAL PORNOGRAPHY

There are three types of pornography that are considered an offence in England and Wales:

1. *Extreme pornography* refers to severely offensive or obscene images and films made for the purpose of sexual arousal. The Criminal Justice and Immigration Act, 2008 in England and Wales considers an offensive and obscene still or moving image as explicit and realistic portrayals of: (1) an act which threatens a person's life; (2) an act which results, or is likely to result, in a serious injury to a person's anus, breasts, or genitals; (3) an act which involves sexual interference with a human corpse or a person performing an act of intercourse or oral sex with an animal (whether dead or alive); (4) an act which involves the non-consensual penetration of a person's vagina, anus, or mouth by another with the other person's penis, other part of their body, or anything else. This Act states that the possession of such extreme pornographic images is an offence.
2. *Disclosing private sexual photographs and films with intent to cause distress, also called "revenge porn"* is an offence in England and Wales under the Criminal Justice and Courts Act, 2015 (Section

33). It is common that those photographs and films are shared by being uploaded on some internet sites. The perpetrator is usually the victim's ex-partner who shares those images or films non-consensually for the purpose to cause distress, humiliation, or embarrassment.

3. *Indecent images of children*. The Protection of Children Act, 1978 states that it is an offence to (1) take, or permit to be taken, or to make, any indecent photograph or pseudo-photograph of a child; (2) distribute or show indecent photographs or pseudo-photographs; (3) to have in possession such indecent photographs or pseudo-photographs, with a view to their being distributed or shown by themselves or others; (4) to publish or cause to be published any advertisement likely to be understood as conveying that the advertiser distributes or shows such indecent photographs or pseudo-photographs, or intends to do so.

SUMMARY

The spectrum of sexualities and sexual behaviours is so wide that it is impossible to classify "normality". However, there are some specific sexual behaviours that are both illegal and considered disorders because they are harmful. What is considered legal or pathological depends on each country's legal, moral, and cultural system. In the UK, some sexual behaviours are considered to be disordered from a psychiatric point of view and to be assessed as such they must cause significant distress or harm to self or others.

Reflective questions:

1 What feelings did reading this chapter generate in you?

2 What has been the most surprising thing to learn?

3 What is the information that is hard for you to accept?

4 Do you know why there are some things that you find hard to accept or read?

5 How is this chapter changing your understanding of sexual normal/abnormal sexual behaviours?

FURTHER READING

Recovery is My Best Revenge. Collected Essays Volumes 1 & 2. My Experience of Trauma, Abuse and Dissociative Disorder, by Caroline Spring (2016).

Rescuing The 'Inner Child'. Therapy for Adults Sexually Abused as Children, by Penny Parks (1990).

Understanding and Addressing Adult Sexual Attraction to Children. A Study of Paedophiles in Contemporary Society, by Sarah D. Goode (2010).

REFERENCES

American Psychiatric Association (APA), (2013). *Diagnostic And Statistical Manual of Mental Disorders*. Fifth Edition (DSM-5). American Psychiatric Publishing. Arlington, VA.

Cantor, J. (n.d.) Website. [Available Online]: http://www.jamescantor.org/downloadables.html

Criminal Justice and Courts Act (2015). Disclosing Private Sexual Photographs and Films with Intent to Cause Distress. [Available Online]: https://www.legislation.gov.uk/ukpga/2015/2/section/33/enacted

Criminal Justice and Immigration Act 2008. Possession of Extreme Pornographic Images. [Available Online]: https://www.legislation.gov.uk/ukpga/2008/4/section/63

Goode, S.D. (2010). *Understanding and Addressing Adult Sexual Attraction to Children. A Study of Paedophiles in Contemporary Society*. Routledge. Abingdon.

Protection of Children Act (1978). Chapter 37: Indecent Photographs of Children. [Available Online]: https://www.legislation.gov.uk/ukpga/1978/37?view=extent

Sexual Offences in UK (2017). [Available Online]: https://www.cps.gov.uk/crime-info/sexual-offences

Shahbaz, C., & Chirinos, P. (2017). *Becoming a Kink Aware Therapist*. Routledge. New York.

The Sexual Offences Act (2003). [Available Online]: https://www.legislation.gov.uk/ukpga/2003/42/contents

UK Government (2022). Consent to Serious Harm [Available Online]: https://www.gov.uk/government/publications/domestic-abuse-bill-2020-factsheets/consent-to-serious-harm-for-sexual-gratification-not-a-defence

SEX IS AN IMPORTANT PART OF OVERALL HEALTH

In the first chapter of this book, I state that sexology is important because it contributes to the full acceptance of human diversity. It contributes to the social justice of protecting our human rights of sexual and relational freedom. Throughout the book, I discuss different dimensions of the important, intimate, and vulnerable aspects of people's lives. Indeed, having knowledge in sexology – and sex education – means that people can conduct their sex lives with better awareness of themselves, including their bodies, and better awareness of others, which in turn increases well-being in sexual health.

Good sexological knowledge does not make people have more sex, it helps people have better quality sex that is pleasure-focused, and safer sex, with full consent and practices to avoid the transmission of sexually transmitted diseases or unwanted pregnancy. It also helps with choosing the right romantic and sexual partner(s) and recognising when a relationship is good or needs improving, based on accurate information. You might think it sounds easy, but in reality it is not because there are so many sex and relationship myths online, on social media, in magazines, and even in books. People are really confused about their sex lives and their relationships, conflicted with so many "shoulds", and often feel bad or ashamed about the intimate parts of their lives because they think they "don't fit" with the myths they read about. Some people even report great distress at feeling such shame or thinking they are "broken". Sexology helps normalise and correct many of those myths, reducing people's distress.

Throughout this book, I have challenged the most common myths regarding sex and relationships because they are the biggest

DOI: 10.4324/9781003276913-11

barriers to good sexual health, and, as you will read in this chapter, overall health.

SEXUAL HEALTH AS PART OF OVERALL HEALTH

The first step is to re-frame our ideas about general health. In the Western world, we tend to prize what is medicalised and we have become more interested in the ideas of "cure". The easier the cure, the better (e.g. taking a pill). Our society has developed to understand the area of health as a synonym to physical health: eating reasonably well, doing moderate exercise, having basic hygiene, brushing our teeth, having a physical health check-up once in a while. All of these are obviously very important, but it is not looking after our overall health because our physical health is only one of the four pillars of health.

The four pillars of health are:

Physical health: the organic, medical aspects of our health, the functioning of our body, our physical health-enhancing lifestyle, which requires good body hygiene.

Mental health: the psychological aspects of our health, how we regulate our emotions and self-compassion, how we think about ourselves, and what behaviours follow, which requires good mental hygiene.

Sexual health: the erotic, sexual pleasure and reproductive aspect of our lives, the careful consideration of consent, the knowledge to avoid disease, which requires good sexual health hygiene.

Spiritual health: the meaning-making aspects of our lives, our sense of belonging, community, and human connection, which requires good philosophical hygiene.

These are not meant to be listed in order of importance. The four pillars of health are equally important and they need to be looked after on a regular basis. In our Western societies, we have managed to separate the four pillars of health in accordance with professional specialisms. A doctor is a specialist in physical health but may have poor training in mental health. A psychotherapist has much knowledge in mental health, but not so much in physical or sexual health. A sexual health specialist has plenty of knowledge of sexually transmitted diseases and the reproductive system, but they may not know as much about the erotic mind. Unfortunately, spiritual health is left aside as something that the "alternative people" are interested in. They are often perceived as the "tree huggers" or religious people, but spiritual health is not necessarily about those things. Although many people find their place of belonging in religion, or in nature, spiritual health is about the fundamental human need for connection, belonging, and meaning-making, whatever form it takes. If we want to re-frame our understanding of health, we need to re-integrate the four pillars of health for ourselves. It means that we have to use our wisdom to know which professionals to approach at any given time.

In my opinion, sexology is the profession that has managed to integrate the four pillars of health with the most success, although there is plenty of room for improvement. This is one of the many reasons why I love sexology so much; it is a truly pluralistic discipline. Our "self" is an intersection of different processes that make up one system. All are intertwined. If one pillar of health is neglected, it affects the other three.

THE HEALTH BENEFITS OF GOOD SEX

Sex is not just what we do, it is an integral part of who we are. Sex is one of the main conduits to experience ourselves with our body and mind, and to express profound and important parts of ourselves. It is a way to connect and relate with others. Sex is not just for procreation or getting an orgasm. As I mentioned in Chapter 6, the study by Meston and Buss (2007) showed that people have sex for 237 reasons.

Some claims such as "frequent sex helps you live longer" are assumed benefits but the scientific data supporting it is debated. Unsurprisingly, most of the scientific research in sexual health is focused on the dysfunctions and preventions of disease and very few focus on the study of the positive, functional, and pleasurable aspects of sex. We do know that there are no health benefits of being abstinent from sex, but it doesn't increase the chances of disease either, therefore it is pretty neutral. Equally, having a lot of sex with multiple partners isn't necessarily the sign of a pathology, but, obviously, there is a higher likelihood of contracting sexually transmitted infections. In most cases, what is definitely psychologically harmful is having a sex life that is incongruent with who we are; for example, someone who is feeling sexual but forces themselves to be abstinent, someone who is gay but forcing themselves to have heterosexual sex, someone who is asexual forcing themselves to have sex.

According to the limited research, here is a brief summary of the reported health benefits associated with sex:

1. *Boosting the immune system.* It is thought that sex can boost our immune system. Although it is important to note that there hasn't been much research about it, one study (Charnetski & Brennan, 2004) suggests that those who had more frequent sex had more immunoglobulin A (IgA), an antibody blood protein that is part of our immune system.

2. *Boosting libido.* The popular saying: "you lose it if you don't use it" appears to be true. More frequent masturbation is associated with higher testosterone, which suggests that it is good for our sex life (Macdowall et al., 2021).

3. *Reduction of prostate cancer.* A study by Rider et al. (2016) confirms that a higher frequency of ejaculation reduces the risk of prostate cancer.

4. *Good for the heart.* A study by Liu et al. (2016) shows that there is a lower level of CRP (C-reactive protein, which measures the levels of inflammation in the body. It is used to find if there is a risk of heart disease) with sexually active men than the sexually inactive men, which seems to suggest that sex is good for the heart. However, older men may have a cardiovascular event with a higher frequency of sex. The study shows that sexual frequency for women has more cardiovascular benefits than for men in older age.

5. *Reduction of blood pressure.* The same study by Liu et al. (2016) also finds that it is not only the sexual activities and frequency that need to be taken into account but also the satisfaction about the sexual activities. Women who expressed satisfaction with their sex lives had lower risks of hypertension. Interestingly, the satisfaction in sex quality does not seem to protect men's cardiovascular health.

6. *Stress relief.* A study by Ditzen et al. (2019) shows that the expression of intimacy lowers cortisol, the stress hormone, when there

is a stressful event. Sex and orgasms release oxytocin and endorphins which also help with reducing stress. This study shows that it is not only sex, but any emotional and physical closeness that reduces cortisol reactivity and accelerates the recovery from stressful events.

7. *Improves sleep.* It appears that orgasms (through partnered sex or masturbation) improve the quality of our sleep (Lastella et al., 2019).

8. *Improves nasal function.* A fascinating study by Bulut et al. (2021) found:

> "sexual intercourse with climax can improve nasal breathing to the same degree as application of nasal decongestant for up to 60 minutes in patients having nasal obstruction".

9. *Sexual intercourse as a form of moderate physical exercise.* A study by Oliva-Lozano et al. (2022) suggests that sexual intercourse could be considered as a moderate physical exercise (depending on several factors including people's health status, intercourse position and duration of the activity). Regular physical exercise is recommended to increase our well-being and avoid health problems. Therefore, regular intercourse could indeed be a fun and pleasurable way to get our physical exercise done, for good health. Equally, Gerbild et al. (2018) found that regular physical exercise helps with improving erections, including "supervised training consisting of 40 minutes of aerobic exercise of moderate to vigorous intensity 4 times per week".

WHAT ABOUT APHRODISIACS?

I'm sure we have all heard of specific foods or products being promoted as aphrodisiacs, giving us the promise of enhancing our sex lives, from oysters, chocolate, honey, and so on. Unfortunately, none of these claims have been clinically proven so it is best to take those stories of aphrodisiacs with a pinch of salt. Some foods and products championed as aphrodisiacs such as "mad honey" might actually be dangerous, so it is best not to believe the sensationalised advertisements and avoid taking such products. Some products such as maca, tribulus, ginkgo, and ginseng have "limited but emerging data" according to a study by West and Krychman (2015). The bottom line is that there are currently no endorsed aphrodisiacs so it is best to look elsewhere for a better sex life. As I have explained in this book, our Erotic Mind is the source of much sex-enhancing experiences.

THE HEALTH BENEFITS OF GOOD RELATIONSHIPS

Sex is not the only important aspect of our lives that have potential health benefits. Good and satisfying relationships do too. Human beings do not do well in isolation, but we don't need a romantic connection to have the health benefits of a good relationship. Any relationships that are loving, caring, supportive, and generous will do (see Chapter 8). Along with that, a study by Thomas and Kim (2021) highlights that non-sexual physical touch such as a hug "links to lower blood pressure, higher oxytocin levels, and better sleep". The COVID-19 pandemic reminded us all of the power of physical touch when some people had less access to others and hugs were banned.

Another study by Lee and Cichy (2020) offers a fascinating report that relationship quality has an impact on older people's cardiovascular risks through touch. People in good quality relationships have lower blood pressure with frequent physical touch. However, people in poor quality relationships have higher blood pressure with frequent physical touch. So, it is good for our health (and heart) if we have lots of physical touch with people we feel comfortable with. But if we happen to be in a poor relationship, we're better off keeping our physical distance!

CHECK YOUR H.A.L.T.O.

The H.A.L.T.O. acronym, developed by Twist and Schoenike (2020), stands for hungry, angry, lonely, tired, and orgasm. The idea is based on Maslow's theory of the hierarchy of needs, which assumes people's basic needs must be met as the foundation of well-being. As we go through life, we can sometimes sustain one basic need not being met for a period of time but when two or more basic needs are not met, people can be destabilised and distressed, with impaired functioning. To keep a balanced life, it is a good idea to learn to check our H.A.L.T.O. on a regular basis:

1. Am I hungry? If so, eat something nutritious and satisfying.
2. Am I angry? If so, take a deep breath, stretch and relax your body or go for a quick walk.
3. Am I lonely? If so, send a text or make a call to a trusted friend, romantic partner, or a good and helpful member of your family.
4. Am I tired? If so, take a break, have a nap, or plan an early night.
5. Am I needing an orgasm? If so, make your orgasm a priority, whether it is partnered or solo sex.

HAPPINESS

In my opinion, "happiness" is a problematic word because it is not something that we can grasp or define. Yet, the pursuit of happiness is intrinsic in our society and the media. Many companies, including a vast amount of therapists, cash in on that concept, selling programmes, "secrets", or techniques to achieve happiness. Hollywood movies, particularly Disney cartoons, perpetuate the myth of "living happily ever after", which consolidates that notion and contributes to making people being pretty unhappy when they realise they are unable to reach that panacea. Unfortunately, rather than questioning the problematic concept of "happiness", people tend to feel bad about themselves for not being able to reach something that they think they should.

The pressure to always be happy or positive actually erodes mental health. In fact, having better mental health is doing the opposite: it is to embrace the uncomfortable idea that we are vulnerable beings, and that it is OK not to be OK, it is OK to hurt, it is OK to fall apart, hide under the duvet and not want to face the world for a few days. Taking the pressure off being happy is taking great care of ourselves and looking after our mental health.

Happiness only happens in fleeting moments of high emotional pleasure. It comes and goes as quickly as an orgasm, or one firework. Instead of trying to reach for happiness, I believe we need to aim for what I call the consistent slow hum of contentment. This is much more achievable for the long term; it is realistic and it is human. The slow hum of contentment is attained when we live our lives in full awareness of ourselves, our sexuality, our intimate world, our relationships and human connections. It is when we can listen to our mind and heart, prioritise what is really important for us, celebrate our eroticism, and honour our bodies. It is when we can quieten the critical, unhelpful voices in our mind, and use our intuition based on our self-awareness to guide us with our inner wisdom.

Happiness is not about forcing ourselves to drink a smoothie and do yoga every day. It is not about making a lot of money. It is not about having the most popular profile on social media. It is not about having our lives "sorted" all the time. It is about being real, human, messy, in full and radical self-acceptance.

SUMMARY

In our Western world, we do not invest much in understanding ourselves, how to choose a good relationship, or adequate sex education, prioritising teachings on economics, career-building, and making profits. Although these disciplines are definitely important to leading a good life and making the world go around, there is a disproportionate lack of interest in the core aspects of our lives that make life a joyous, pleasurable, and health-enhancing experience. Our self-awareness, our relationships, our erotic lives, our passions, and our sense of belonging are very important.

Sexology is crucial to our overall health because it encompasses our physical health, mental health, sexual health, and spiritual health. Learning to have good intimate relationships and erotic awareness helps us to attain consistent contentment and experience fleeting happiness.

Reflective questions:

1 What are the health-enhancing factors that you need more of?

2 What can contribute to improving your relationship(s), including your friendships?

3 Are there some people you feel you have to meet out of duty but actually don't enjoy spending time with? If so, what can you do to change that situation, for your health?

4 What does contentment look like for you? What do you need to address to attain it?

5 What are the important learnings you have made about your sexuality, erotic world, and intimate relationships when reading this book?

FURTHER READING

Come As You Are. The Surprising New Science that Will Transform Your Sex Life, by Emily Nagoski (2015).

Mating In Captivity. Unlocking Erotic Intelligence, by Esther Perel (2006).

Transforming Sexual Narratives: A Relational Approach to Sex Therapy, by Suzanne Iasenza (2020).

REFERENCES

Bulut, O.C., Oladokun, D., Lippert, B.M., & Hohenberger, R. (2021). Can Sex Improve Nasal Function?—An Exploration of the Link Between Sex and Nasal Function. *Ear, Nose & Throat Journal*. doi:10.1177/0145561320981441

Charnetski, C.J., & Brennan, F.X. (2004). Sexual Frequency and Salivary Immunoglobulin A (IgA). *Psychological Reports*, 94(3), 839–844. doi:10.2466/pr0.94.3.839-844

Ditzen, B., Germann, J., Meuwly, N., Bradbury, T., Bodenmann, G., & Heinrichs, M. (2019). Intimacy as Related to Cortisol Reactivity and Recovery in Couples Undergoing Psychosocial Stress. *Psychosomatic Medicine*, Jan, 81(1), 16–25. doi:10.1097/PSY.0000000000000633

Gerbild, H., Larsen, C.M., Graugaard, C., Areskoug Josefsson, K. (2018). Physical Activity to Improve Erectile Function: A Systematic Review of Intervention Studies. Sexual medicine, Jun, 6(2), 75–89. doi: 10.1016/j.esxm.2018.02.001.

Lastella, M., O'Mullan, C., Paterson, J.L., & Reynolds, A.C. (2019). Sex and Sleep: Perceptions of Sex as a Sleep Promoting Behavior in the General Adult Population. *Front Public Health*, Mar 4, 7, 33. doi:10.3389/fpubh.2019.00033. PMID: 30886838; PMCID: PMC6409294.

Lee, J.E., & Cichy, K.E. (2020). Complex Role of Touch in Social Relationships for Older Adults' Cardiovascular Disease Risk. *Research on Aging*, 42(7–8), 208–216. doi:10.1177/0164027520915793

Liu, H., Waite, L.J., Shen, S., & Wang, D.H. (2016). Is Sex Good for Your Health? A National Study on Partnered Sexuality and Cardiovascular Risk among Older Men and Women. *Journal of Health and Social Behavior*, 57(3), 276–296. doi:10.1177/0022146516661597

Macdowall, W.G., Clifton, S., Palmer, M.J., Tanton, C., Copas, A.J., Lee, D.M., Mitchell, K.R., Mercer, C.H., Sonnenberg, P., Johnson A.M., & Wellings, K. (2021) Salivary Testosterone and Sexual Function and Behavior in Men and

Women: Findings from the Third British National Survey of Sexual Attitudes and Lifestyles (Natsal-3). *The Journal of Sex Research.* doi:10.1080/00224499. 2021.1968327

Meston, C.M., & Buss, D.M. (2007). Why Humans Have Sex. *Archives of Sexual Behavior*, 36, 477–507. doi:10.1007/s10508-007-9175-2

Oliva-Lozano, J.M., Alacid, F., López-Miñarro, P.A., & Muyor J.M. (2022). What Are the Physical Demands of Sexual Intercourse? A Systematic Review of the Literature. *Archives of Sexual Behavior*, 51, 1397–1417. doi:10.1007/s10508-021-02246-8

Rider, J.R., Wilson, K.M., Sinnott, J.A., Kelly, R.S., Mucci, L.A., & Giovannucci, E.L. (2016). Ejaculation Frequency and Risk of Prostate Cancer: Updated Results with an Additional Decade of Follow-up. *European Urology*, Dec, 70(6), 974–982. doi:10.1016/j.eururo.2016.03.027. Epub 2016 Mar 28. PMID: 27033442; PMCID: PMC5040619.

Thomas, P.A., & Kim, S. (2021). Lost Touch? Implications of Physical Touch for Physical Health. *The Journals of Gerontology: Series B*, March, 76(3), e111–e115. doi:10.1093/geronb/gbaa134

Twist, M.L.C., & Schoenike, C.J. (2020). Hungry? Angry? Lonely? Tired? Orgasmed?: H.A.L.T.O. Check. *The MFT Courier*, 35(1), 7–10. [Available Online]: https://www.academia.edu/44471415/University_of_Wisconsin_Stout_Marriage_and_Family_Therapy_Program

West, E., & Krychman, M. (2015). Natural Aphrodisiacs-A Review of Selected Sexual Enhancers. *Sexual Medicine Reviews*, Oct, 3(4), 279–288. doi:10.1002/smrj.62. Epub 2015 Nov 10. PMID: 27784600.

CONCLUSION

Sexology is a relatively young professional field but is rooted in central themes that have existed for as long as human beings have existed: sex, desire, eroticism, fantasies, diverse sexual practices, emotional connections, intimate relationships, attachments, and love. Human beings have pondered, made art, and written about those themes for centuries because they represent a profound and meaningful existential element of who we are as people. Through the study of sexology, much of the human experience is normalised, moving further away from the language of pathology and dysfunctions to one of acceptance of differences and colourful diversities: the different genders, the wide range of sexual orientations, the vast world of eroticism, the multiple intersections of each person's unique experiencing of their own body, mind, sexual behaviours and the shape that our intimate relationships take. Adopting the broad view of gender, sexuality and relationship diversity allows us to be much more aware of who we are, enables us to access our erotic and relational wisdom, and gives us clarity to make a fully informed consensual choice with our sex lives and relationships, and, ultimately, it helps us be kinder to ourselves and each other.

DOI: 10.4324/9781003276913-12

INDEX

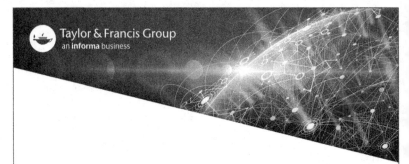

Printed in the United States
by Baker & Taylor Publisher Services